SPANISH

Verbs

& Essentials of Grammar

Second Edition

Ina Ramboz

Mc
Graw
Hill

New York   Chicago   San Francisco   Lisbon   London   Madrid   Mexico City
Milan   New Delhi   San Juan   Seoul   Singapore   Sydney   Toronto

1 2 3 4 5 6 7 8 9 10 11 12 13 14 15 16 17 18 19   CUS/CUS   0 9 8 7

ISBN 978-0-07-149806-7
MHID   0-07-149806-0

This book is printed on acid-free paper.

Preface

This new edition of *Spanish Verbs and Essentials of Grammar* presents the major grammatical concepts of the Spanish language in accordance with the Spanish Royal Academy.

As evidenced by the first section of this book, major emphasis is given to the mastery of verbs, their conjugations and uses. Grammar and sentence structure are presented in contexts easily understood. A spiraling approach is used in such a way that new items are introduced through and built upon material that has previously been learned. Each grammatical point has been introduced in concise segments to enable the student to fully grasp each section under study.

The advantage of *Spanish Verbs and Essentials of Grammar* is that, contrary to the majority of foreign language textbooks, the complete grammatical explanations are contained in one section. Topics are not scattered throughout the text; teacher and student can easily find specific information required.

Following each grammatical or verbal explanation are numerous examples. These provide the teacher or student with necessary illustrations. The synopses and tables of verb endings facilitate reference work and the learning of individual tenses as well as providing contrasting elements. The lists of verbs and vocabularies of related words and phrases provide material which may be used for creative exercises, compositions, or oral practice, review or pronunciation practice.

As a reference text, *Spanish Verbs and Essentials of Grammar* can be used by the individual student for study or review, or by the teacher and the class as a supplement to any of the basal textbooks. This new edition can save time for the student by eliminating the need to write lengthy grammatical explanations in a notebook. It can serve the teacher as a supplementary source guide. Because of the logical order of presentation of concepts, this book can be used on any level, from junior high school through college, as well as for adults in a refresher course or in business.

For additional practice and reinforcement of verb conjugations and tenses, readers may wish to consult *Spanish Verb Drills,* which appears in the listing at the end of this book together with various Passport titles in Spanish and other languages.

Contents

Part One: Spanish Verbs

Part Two: Essentials of Grammar

Part One:
Spanish Verbs

1. Pronunciation

The Alphabet

The Spanish alphabet contains 26 simple and 1 compound letter. W *(doble u)* can be added but usually only appears in foreign words, as does the *k*. The compound letter *rr* is never separated and never begins a word. The letters are all feminine.

a	*a*	h	*hache*	ñ	*eñe*	t	*te*
b	*be*	i	*i*	o	*o*	u	*u*
c	*ce*	j	*jota*	p	*pe*	v	*ve*
d	*de*	k	*ka*	q	*cu*	x	*equis*
e	*e*	l	*ele*	r	*ere*	y	*ye, i griega*
f	*efe*	m	*eme*	rr	*erre*	z	*zeta*
g	*ge*	n	*ene*	s	*ese*		

A mayúscula	capital A	˜(ñ)	*la tilde* tilde
a minúscula	small a	¨(ü)	*la diéresis, la crema,*
á el acento	accent		dieresis

The approximate pronunciation of each letter is like that found in the English word that follows it.

Vowels

a ah: *padre, sala*
e they: *me, mesa, leche*
   When *e* is followed by a consonant in the same syllable, it sounds like the *e* in tell: *el, te-ner, a-fec-to.*
i machine: *mi, tinta*
o note: *no, nota*
   When *o* is followed by a consonant in same syllable, it sounds like *o* in or: *por, flor*
u rule: *uno, luna*

Consonants

b, v, boy
   Like *b* in boy when initial in a breath group and after *m* and *n:* *basta, burro, voy, ver, hombre, invierno*
   Between vowels the lips are more relaxed, scarcely touching each other: *Cuba, saber, uva, lavar*

3

*c Before *a, o, u,* or a consonant, as in cat: *cama, como, cuna, claro*
Before *e, i,* like *c* in city: *cena, cine*
ch child: *chico, mucho*
d When initial, somewhat like the *d* in day but with the tip of the tongue placed on the lower edge of the upper teeth rather than on the upper part: *día, dama.* At the end of a word or between vowels, like *th* in than: *Madrid, verdad, nada, pasado*
f fine: *fino, final*
g Before *a, o, u,* or a consonant, like *g* in go: *gato, goma, gusto, gloria*
Also in the syllables *gue, gui:* (the *u* is not sounded unless it has the dieresis) *guerra, guitarra, vergüenza*
Between vowels the sound is softer: *agua, amigo*
Before *e, i,* like *h* in here: *gente, gitano*
h Silent
j Like *h* in here: *José, jugo*
k kind: *kilo*
l like: *libro, letra*
ll like *y* in beyond: *calle, pollo*
m my: *mi, madre*
n name: *no, nada*
ñ union: *niño, señor*
p pay: *padre, pasar*
q Like *k,* but found only in the syllables *que, qui,* the *u* not sounded: *queso, aquí, quitar*
r Lightly trilled with the tip of the tongue: *pero, caro*
When initial or after *l* or *n,* it is strongly trilled: *Rosa, repita, alrededor, Enrique.*
rr Strongly trilled: *burro, perro, carro*
s Usually as in same: *suma, casa*
Before *b, d, g, l, m, n,* somewhat like the *s* in rose: *desde, mismo*
t tea: *tanto, tinta*
w will: Washington
x Between vowels like *x* in tax: *examen, éxito*
Before a consonant, like *s: extranjero, extremo*
y As a consonant (at the beginning, or within a word) like *y* in yes: *yo, ayer*
When standing alone as a conjunction or at the end of a word, like the vowel *i: Juan y María, rey, Paraguay.*
*z Like *c* in city: *zapato, azul, vez*

*In parts of Spain *c* before *e* or *i* is pronounced like *th* in thin; *ll* like *lli* in million; *z* like *th* in thin.

Accent or Stress

In words ending in a vowel, *n,* or *s,* stress the next to the last syllable (**ca**ma, **li**bro). In words ending in a consonant (co**mer**, vi**vir**) (except *n* or *s*) (**ca**mas, **co**men) stress the last syllable. If a word has a written accent it shows that the stress does not conform to these rules.

The accent is used to distinguish words that are spelled alike: *el,* the; *él,* he.

A word has as many syllables as it has vowels, diphthongs or triphthongs. Whenever possible each syllable should end in a vowel: *bo-ni-to, se-ño-ri-ta, e-lla.*

In general, the combinations of inseparable consonants are the same as in English except that *s* does not go with a following consonant. Prefixes are inseparable: *li-bro, ex-pli-ca, cas-ti-gar, a-tar, des-a-tar*

Diphthongs, Triphthongs

The strong vowels are *a, e,* and *o; u* and *i* are weak vowels. Strong vowels are separated and can form separate syllables: *po-e-ma, le-e, ro-de-o, ca-no-a.*

The combination of a strong and a weak vowel or two weak ones, forms a diphthong, and may not be separated unless the weak one bears a written accent: *bai-le, cau-sa, fa-mi-lia, a-le-grí-a, ba-úl.*

In a diphthong composed of a strong and a weak vowel the strong one is stressed. In a diphthong composed of two weak vowels the last one is stressed: *oi-ga, cria-da, rui-do, triun-fo.*

The combination of a strong vowel between two weak ones forms a triphthong and may not be separated. The strong one is stressed. When a verb ending bears an accent, it is retained: *Pa-ra-guay, es-tu-diáis.*

Y at the end of a word, although having the sound of a vowel, is considered a consonant in regard to stress.

Punctuation Marks

,	la coma	( )	el paréntesis
.	el punto final	« »	las comillas
:	dos puntos	'	el apóstrofo
;	el punto y coma	-	el guión
. . .	los puntos suspensivos	—	la raya
¿?	los signos de interrogación		
¡!	los signos de admiración		

Punctuation in Spanish, although much the same as in English, has the following differences:

1. An inverted interrogation or exclamation point is placed at the beginning of a question or an exclamation, in addition to the regular form placed at the end.

Juan, ¿qué hace usted?   John, what are you doing?
¡Qué interesante!   How interesting!

2. The dash is used to set off the words of the different speakers in a dialogue. Quotation marks are used for all other quotations and to indicate thought.

—¿Cuándo va?— le preguntó. "When are you going?" he asked.

—Mañana— dijo Carlos. "Tomorrow," said Charles.
Al verlo, pensó: ≪ ¡Es mara- On seeing it, he thought, "It is
villoso! ≫ marvelous!"

3. The apostrophe is used only to indicate the omission of a letter.

¿Qu' es eso? for ¿Qué es eso? What is that?

2. Regular Verbs— Indicative Tenses

Subject Pronouns

The subject of a verb is of first, second, or third person, singular or plural. The speaker is called the first person; the one addressed, the second person; and the one spoken of, the third person.

	Singular		Plural	
1.	**yo** I	1.	**nosotros** (m.)	we
			nosotras (f.)	
2.	**tú** you	2.	**vosotros** (m.)	you
			vosotras (f.)	
	usted you		**ustedes**	you
3.	**él** he	3.	**ellos** (m.)	they
	ella she		**ellas** (f.)	

Usted (ustedes), called the polite form of you, is the one commonly used, and corresponds to the ordinary English you. It is derived from the old form of address, *vuestra merced* (*vuestras mercedes*), your grace, which it now replaces. It may be abbreviated *Ud.* or *Uds.*

Tú (*vosotros, -as*), called the familiar form of you, is used in the family, among intimate friends, or when speaking to children, servants and animals and is used in poetry, prayer and the Bible.

Conjugations

All Spanish verbs end in *-ar, -er,* or *-ir.* This form is called the infinitive.

*habl***ar**, to speak   *com***er**, to eat   *viv***ir**, to live

Verbs are classed as verbs of the first, second, or third conjugation according to the ending of the infinitive. What remains of the verb when the ending is removed is called the stem.

The sets of endings which are added to the stem or to the infinitive to denote person, number, tense, and mood are called conjugations.

Simple Tenses of the Indicative Mood

1. Present	1. *Presente*
2. Imperfect	2. *Imperfecto*
3. Preterite	3. *Pretérito*
4. Future	4. *Futuro*
5. Conditional	5. *Condicional*

First Conjugation, -ar

The Present

The present tense expresses an uncompleted action or state and is formed by adding the endings to the stem of the infinitive.

hablar, to speak
I speak, do speak, am speaking; you speak, etc.

	Singular			Plural	
1. yo	habl*o*	I speak	1. nosotros / nosotras	habl*amos*	we speak
2. tú	habl*as*	you speak	2. vosotros / vosotras	habl*áis*	you speak
usted	habl*a*	you speak	ustedes	habl*an*	you speak
3. él	habl*a*	he speaks	3. ellos	habl*an*	they speak
ella	habl*a*	she speaks	ellas	habl*an*	they speak

Subject pronouns are usually omitted except when needed for clearness or emphasis.

Hablo español.	I speak Spanish.
Hablamos inglés.	We speak English.
Usted **habla español muy bien.**	You speak Spanish very well.
El **habla francés.**	He speaks French.
Ella **habla portugués.**	She speaks Portuguese.

A noun, or a combination of a noun and a pronoun, may be used as the subject of some of the verb forms.

Alberto **habla italiano.**	Albert speaks Italian.
Los alumnos **hablan inglés.**	The pupils speak English.
Juan y yo **hablamos español.**	John and I speak Spanish.
El y su padre **hablan alemán.**	He and his father speak German.

It, understood, may also be the subject of a verb in the third person singular. This happens when the noun for which it stands is not repeated.

El tranvía pasa por aquí. Pasa cada diez minutos.	The street car passes by here. It passes every ten minutes.

Negative Form

To form the negative, place *no* before the verb.

Yo *no* **hablo muy bien.**	I do not speak very well.
Antonio *no* **habla inglés.**	Anthony does not speak English.

Interrogative Form

To form a question, simply place the subject after the verb.

Do or does (when used as an auxiliary) is always understood and never expressed.

¿Habla *usted* francés?	Do you speak French?
¿Qué habla *ella*?	What does she speak?
¿Habla *Juan* inglés?	Does John speak English?

Sample Verbs of the First Conjugation

bajar	to go down, to lower	**limpiar**	to clean
borrar	to erase	**nadar**	to swim
cantar	to sing	**necesitar**	to need
comprar	to buy	**pasar**	to pass; to happen
cortar	to cut	**pesar**	to weigh
dictar	to dictate	**pintar**	to paint
enseñar	to show; to teach	**plantar**	to plant
entrar (en)	to enter	**preparar**	to prepare
estudiar	to study	**pronunciar**	to pronounce
ganar	to earn; to win	**terminar**	to finish
gastar	to spend	**tomar**	to take
gritar	to shout	**trabajar**	to work
hablar	to speak, to talk	**usar**	to use
lavar	to wash	**viajar**	to travel

Note: About 90% of all Spanish verbs end in -ar.

Second Conjugation, -*er*

comer, to eat
I eat, do eat, am eating; you eat, etc.

Singular	Plural
yo com*o*	nosotros(as) com*emos*
tú com*es*	vosotros(as) com*éis*
usted⎫	ustedes⎫
él⎬com*e*	ellos⎬com*en*
ella⎭	ellas⎭

Yo *como* **pan.**	I eat bread.
Juan no *come* **carne.**	John does not eat meat.
¿*Come* **Ud. fruta?**	Do you eat fruit?
Los niños *comen* **dulces.**	The children eat candy.
Comemos **en el comedor.**	We eat in the dining room.

Sample Verbs of the Second Conjugation

aprender	to learn	**deber**	to owe; ought, should
barrer	to sweep	**esconder**	to hide
beber	to drink	**meter**	to put, put in
comer	to eat	**prometer**	to promise
comprender	to understand	**responder**	to respond, answer
correr	to run	**toser**	to cough
coser	to sew	**vender**	to sell

Third Conjugation, -*ir*

vivir, to live
I live, do live, am living; you live, etc.

Singular	Plural
yo viv*o*	nosotros(as) viv*imos*
tú viv*es*	vosotros(as) viv*ís*
Ud.⎫	Uds.⎫
él ⎬viv*e*	ellos ⎬viv*en*
ella⎭	ellas ⎭

Yo *vivo* **en la ciudad.**	I live in the city.
Juan *vive* **en el campo.**	John lives in the country.
¿Dónde *vive* **Ud.?**	Where do you live?
Vivimos **en América.**	We live in America.
Ellos *viven* **en México.**	They live in Mexico.

Sample Verbs of the Third Conjugation

*abrir to open	*describir to describe
aplaudir to applaud	invadir to invade
asistir (a) to attend	omitir to omit
combatir to fight	recibir to receive
*cubrir to cover	subir to go up, to carry up
*descubrir to discover	sufrir to suffer
*escribir to write	vivir to live

*Note: Regular except in past participle

Present Tense Sentences

Juan *trabaja* **en una tienda.**	John works in a store.
María *limpia* **la casa.**	Mary cleans the house.
Alicia *cose* **muy bien.**	Alice sews very well.
¿Qué *escribe* **Ud.?**	What are you writing?
Juan *abre* **las ventanas.**	John opens the windows.
¿*Necesita* **Ud. un libro?**	Do you need a book?
Los niños *beben* **leche.**	The children drink milk.
Nadamos **en el río.**	We swim in the river.
Los niños *corren* **y** *gritan.*	The children run and shout.
Prometo **estudiar más.**	I promise to study more.

The Imperfect

There are two past tenses in Spanish, the imperfect and the preterite. Their uses vary.

The imperfect is used to express an action or state as going on in the past, as repeated or habitual.

It is also used for description, either of physical conditions or mental states.

The imperfect tense is formed by adding the endings to the stem of the infinitive.

hablar, I was speaking, used to speak; you were speaking, etc.

hablaba	hablábamos
hablabas	hablabais
hablaba	hablaban

comer		vivir	
I was eating, etc.		I was living, etc.	
comía	comíamos	vivía	vivíamos
comías	comíais	vivías	vivías
comía	comían	vivía	vivían

Juan hablaba de su viaje.	John was talking of his trip.
María cosía todos los días.	Mary used to sew every day.
Yo vivía en España.	I used to live in Spain.
La niña tenía los ojos azules.	The child had blue eyes.
Luisa estaba triste.	Louise was sad.

The Preterite

The preterite tense expresses an action or state completed in the past. The auxiliary did is always understood.

The preterite tense is formed by adding the endings to the stem of the infinitive.

hablar		comer		vivir	
I spoke, did speak, etc.		I ate, did eat, etc.		I lived, etc.	
hablé	hablamos	comí	comimos	viví	vivimos
hablaste	hablasteis	comiste	comisteis	viviste	vivisteis
habló	hablaron	comió	comieron	vivió	vivieron

Ayer *hablé* con su madre.	Yesterday I talked with his mother.
Viví en España dos años.	I lived in Spain two years.
¿*Compró* Ud. el libro?	Did you buy the book?
¿*Vendieron* la casa?	Did they sell the house?
¿Quién *comió* la fruta?	Who ate the fruit?
Ernesto escribía cuando yo *entré*.	Ernest was writing when I entered.

The Future

The future tense has but one set of endings for all three conjugations. The endings are added the whole infinitive.

hablar		comer		vivir	
I shall speak, etc.		I shall eat, etc.		I shall live, etc.	
hablaré	hablaremos	comeré	comeremos	viviré	viviremos
hablarás	hablaréis	comerás	comeréis	vivirás	viviréis
hablará	hablarán	comerá	comerán	vivirá	vivirán

1. The tense usually expresses future time (I shall —, he will —).

Hablaré **español con María.**	I shall speak Spanish with Mary.
José *escribirá* **la carta.**	Joseph will write the letter.
Aprenderán **los verbos.**	They will learn the verbs.

2. The future is also used to express probability or conjecture, referring to the present.

¿Dónde *estará* **mi libro?**	Where can my book be?
Estará **en casa.**	It is probably at home.

The Conditional

The endings for the conditional tense are the same for all three conjugations. They are added to the whole infinitive.

hablar	**com**er	**viv**ir
I would speak,	I would eat, etc.	I would live, etc.
you would speak, etc.		

hablar*ía*	**hablar***íamos*	**comer***ía*	**comer***íamos*	**vivir***ía*	**vivir***íamos*
hablar*ías*	**hablar***íais*	**comer***ías*	**comer***íais*	**vivir***ías*	**vivir***íais*
hablar*ía*	**hablar***ían*	**comer***ía*	**comer***ían*	**vivir***ía*	**vivir***ían*

1. The conditional tense often expresses an idea dependent on a condition, either expressed or understood (I would —, he would —).

Yo *hablaría* **español.**	I would speak Spanish. (if I were in Spain)
¿*Compraría* **Ud. la casa?**	Would you buy the house?
Teniendo el dinero, la *compraría.*	Having (if I had) the money, I would buy it.
Juan dijo que *aprendería* **los verbos.**	John said that he would learn the verbs.
María dijo que *escribiría.*	Mary said that she would write.

2. The conditional also expresses probability or conjecture, referring to the past.

Rosa *estaría* **enferma.**	Rose was probably ill.
Llegarían **anoche.**	They probably arrived last night.

Endings of Simple Tenses of the Indicative

	—ar	—er	—ir	
Present	stem o __amos	__o __emos	__o __imos	
	__as __áis	__es __éis	__es __ís	
	__a __an	__e __en	__e __en	

am, are, is, do, does —

	— ar	—er, —ir	
Imperfect	__aba __ábamos	__ía __íamos	used to,
	__abas __abais	__ías __íais	was ___
	__aba __aban	__ía __ían	

	—ar	—er, —ir	
Preterite	__é __amos	__í __imos	
	__aste __asteis	__iste __isteis	did___
	__ó __aron	__ió __ieron	

	—ar, —er, —ir		
Future	infinitive é __emos		shall,
	__ás __éis		will___
	__á __án		

	—ar, —er, —ir		
Conditional	infinitive ía __íamos		
	__ías __íais		would___
	__ía __ían		

Verb Synopsis

In a synopsis any one form of the verb is given in all the tenses.

hablar—yo

Indicative	Simple Tenses	Translation
Present	**hablo**	I speak
Imperfect	**hablaba**	I used to speak
Preterite	**hablé**	I spoke
Future	**hablaré**	I shall speak
Conditional	**hablaría**	I would speak

Note: For regular verbs, see pages 9, 10. The illustrative sentences (pages 8, 9, 10) may be used as exercises by changing the tense of the verbs, or by writing them in the form of a synopsis.

3. Perfect Tenses of the Indicative

The perfect tenses, which are compound, are formed by using the five simple tenses of the auxiliary verb *haber,* to have, with a past participle.

Past Participle

A past participle is formed by adding *-ado* to the stem of *-ar* verbs, and *-ido* to the stem of *-er* and *-ir* verbs.

habl*ar*	habl*ado*	spoken
com*er*	com*ido*	eaten
viv*ir*	viv*ido*	lived

The perfect tenses are as follows:

1. Present Perfect	*Perfecto*
2. Past Perfect (Pluperfect)	*Pluscuamperfecto*
3. Preterite Perfect	*Pretérito perfecto*
4. Future Perfect	*Futuro perfecto*
5. Conditional Perfect	*Condicional perfecto*

Present Perfect

The present perfect is formed with the present of *haber* and a past participle. (have or has —)

hablar, I have spoken, you have spoken, he has spoken, etc.

he	hablado	hemos	hablado
has	hablado	habéis	hablado
ha	hablado	han	hablado

He hablado con su padre.	I have talked with his father.
No *han vendido* la casa.	They have not sold the house.
¿*Ha comido* Ud. los dulces?	Have you eaten the candy?

There are two past perfect tenses in Spanish, the *pluscuamperfecto* and the *pretérito perfecto.* They are formed with the two past tenses of *haber,* and have the same meaning but they are used differently. The past perfect that is used most often is the one that follows immediately.

Past Perfect

This tense is formed with the imperfect of *haber* + a past participle. (had—)

hablar, I had spoken, you had spoken, he had spoken, etc.

había	hablado	habíamos	hablado
habías	hablado	habíais	hablado
había	hablado	habían	hablado

Juan dijo que *había hablado* **español con Carlos.**	John said that he had spoken Spanish with Charles.
Carlos *había vivido* **en México.**	Charles had lived in Mexico.
Allí *había aprendido* **el español.**	There he had learned Spanish.

Preterite Perfect

This tense is formed with the preterite of *haber* + a past participle. (had—)

hablar, I had spoken, you had spoken, etc.

hube	hablado	hubimos	hablado
hubiste	hablado	hubisteis	hablado
hubo	hablado	hubieron	hablado

This tense has the same meaning as the *pluscuamperfecto,* but it is used only after conjunctions of time, such as:

así que			**cuando** when
luego que	}	as soon as	**después (de) que** after
tan pronto como			**hasta que** until

Después que *hubo hablado* **con Juan, salió del cuarto.**	After he had talked with John, he left the room.
Luego que *hube entrado* **en la sala, la vi.**	As soon as I had entered the room, I saw her.

Future Perfect

The future perfect is formed with the future of *haber* + a past participle. (shall have—, will have—)

hablar, I shall have spoken, you will have spoken, etc.

habré	hablado	habremos	hablado
habrás	hablado	habréis	hablado
habrá	hablado	habrán	hablado

Le *habré hablado* **antes de la llegada de Ud.**
I shall have spoken to him before your arrival.
Habré aprendido **los verbos para mañana.**
I shall have learned the verbs by tomorrow.

Note: The future perfect is also used to express probability or conjecture, referring to the present.

Habrán llegado.	They have probably arrived.
Habrá hablado **de su hijo.**	He has probably spoken of his son.

Conditional Perfect

The conditional perfect is formed with the conditional of *haber* + a past participle. (would have—)

hablar, I would have spoken, you would have spoken, etc.

habría	hablado	habríamos	hablado
habrías	hablado	habríais	hablado
habría	hablado	habrían	hablado

Yo no *habría hablado* **del asunto sin consultarle.**	I would not have spoken of the matter without consulting him.
¿Lo *habría vendido* **Ud.?**	Would you have sold it?

Note: The conditional perfect is also used to express probability or conjecture, referring to the past.

Habrían llegado.	They had probably arrived.
Lo *habría visto.*	He had probably seen it.

Irregular Past Participles

abrir to open	**abierto**	**hacer** to do, make	**hecho**
cubrir to cover	**cubierto**	**morir** to die	**muerto**
descubrir to discover	**descubierto**	**poner** to put, place	**puesto**
decir to say	**dicho**	**romper** to break	**roto**
escribir to write	**escrito**	**ver** to see	**visto**
describir to describe	**descrito**	**volver** to return	**vuelto**

Perfect Tenses of the Indicative

haber + —past participle

Present Perfect	he___	hemos___	have___
	has___	habéis___	or
Perfecto	ha___	han___	has___
Past Perfect	había___	habíamos___	
	habías___	habíais___	had___
Pluscuamperfecto	había___	habían___	
Preterite Perfect	hube___	hubimos___	
	hubiste___	hubisteis___	had___
Pretérito perfecto	hubo___	hubieron___	
Future Perfect	habré___	habremos___	shall have___
	habrás___	habréis___	or
Futuro perfecto	habrá___	habrán___	will have___
Conditional Perfect	habría___	habríamos___	
	habrías___	habríais___	would have___
Condicional perfecto	habría___	habrían___	

Synopsis of the Perfect Tenses

hablar —yo

Present Perfect	he hablado	I have spoken.
Past Perfect	había hablado	I had spoken.
Preterite Perfect	hube hablado	I had spoken.
Future Perfect	habré hablado	I shall have spoken.
Conditional Perfect	habría hablado	I would have spoken.

4. Reflexive Verbs

A reflexive verb is one whose subject and object are the same; that is, the subject acts upon itself. The verb is always used with some form of the reflexive pronouns. A reflexive verb is indicated by the pronoun *se* attached to the infinitive.

levantar*se*, to rise
Present

I rise (raise myself), you rise (raise yourself), etc.

(yo) *me* levanto	(nosotros, -as) *nos* levantamos
(tú) *te* levantas	(vosotros, -as) *os* levantáis
(Ud., él, ella) *se* levanta	(Uds., ellos, ellas) *se* levantan

Position of the Reflexive Pronoun

The reflexive pronoun precedes a conjugated verb except in a direct affirmative command, when it follows and is attached to it. It precedes another object pronoun. It follows and is attached to an infinitive or a gerund.

Juan *se* levanta a las seis.	John rises at six o'clock.
No *se* levantará tarde.	He will not rise late.
Levánte*se* Ud. temprano.	Rise early.
No *se* levante tarde.	Do not rise late.
El no quiere levantar*se*.	He does not want to rise.
Ya está levantándo*se*. } Ya *se* está levantando.}	Now he is rising.
Se lo puso.	He put it on.

Note: When the reflexive pronouns *nos* and *os* are joined to the verb, the final letter of the latter is dropped.

Levantemos + nos = Levantémonos   Levantad + os = Levant*aos*

Exception: **irse   idos,** Go away.

The meaning of many verbs varies according to the form.

acostar(ue)	to put to bed	**acostarse**	to go to bed
bañar	to bathe	**bañarse**	to bathe oneself
casar	to marry	**casarse**	to get married

despertar(ie) to awaken someone	**despertarse** to wake up
ir to go	**irse** to go away
levantar to raise	**levantarse** to rise
sentar(ie) to seat	**sentarse** to sit down
tratar(de) to treat, try	**tratarse de** to treat of
vestir(i) to dress	**vestirse** to dress oneself

Some verbs are always used in the reflexive form.

arrepentirse(ie) to repent	**dignarse** to deign
atreverse to dare	**jactarse** to boast
desayunarse to eat breakfast	**quejarse** to complain

Reciprocal Verbs

A reflexive verb is called reciprocal when the action passes from one person or thing to another, or from one group to another. It is only used in the first and third persons plural.

Se **miran.**	They look at each other.
Nos **ayudamos.**	We help each other.

Since a reciprocal construction may have two meanings, ambiguity is avoided by adding the forms: *el uno al otro, la una a la otra, unos a otros*, etc., or the words *mismos, -as.*

Se **miraban** *el uno al otro.*	They were looking at each other.
Se **aborrecen** *la una a la otra.*	They hate each other.
Nos **ayudamos a** *nosotros mismos.*	We help ourselves.
Se **engañan a** *sí mismos.*	They deceive themselves.
Se **hablaron** *la una a la otra.*⎫ *Se* **hablaron** *unos a otros.* ⎭	They talked to each other.

5. Tenses of the Subjunctive Mood

There are four tenses of the subjunctive in common use. An old form, the future subjunctive, is now rarely used.

Subjunctive Tenses

1. Present	*Presente*
2. Past	*Imperfecto*
3. Present Perfect	*Perfecto*
4. Past Perfect	*Pretérito perfecto*

Present Subjunctive

The regular present subjunctive is formed by adding the endings to the stem of the infinitive (may —).

hab*lar*	com*er*	viv*ir*
I may speak,	I may eat, you	I may live, you
you may speak, etc.	may eat, etc.	may live, etc.

hab*le*	hab*lemos*	com*a*	com*amos*	viv*a*	viv*amos*
hab*les*	hab*léis*	com*as*	com*áis*	viv*as*	viv*áis*
hab*le*	hab*len*	com*a*	com*an*	viv*a*	viv*an*

The present subjunctive is translated in many ways according to how it is used. Many times it is translated as may—, expressing possibility or uncertainty. This is often true when used after the adverbs *quizás, tal vez, acaso,* perhaps, and also in many dependent clauses. The specific uses of the subjunctive will be discussed in the next chapter.

Quizás me *escriba.*	Perhaps he may write to me.
Tal vez *hable* **de su viaje.**	Perhaps he may talk of his trip.
Le doy el libro para que *estudie.*	I give him the book in order that he may study.
Lo haré aunque *sea* **difícil.**	I shall do it, although it may be difficult.
Lo buscaré aunque no lo *halle.*	I shall look for it, although I may not find it.

Commands

The present subjunctive is also used in commands with *Ud.* and *Uds.* With *tú* and *vosotros,* it is used only in negative commands. These will be discussed in detail in a later chapter.

Hable **Ud. español.**	**No hable Ud. inglés.**
Speak Spanish.	Do not speak English.
No *hables* **tú.**	**No habléis vosotros.**
Do not speak.	Do not speak.

Position of object pronouns with a command

In a command the subject, if expressed, follows the verb. The object pronoun follows and is attached to the verb if affirmative, but placed before it if negative.

Coma *Ud.* **la fruta.**	**Cóma***la* **Ud.**	**No** *la* **coma Ud.**
Eat the fruit.	Eat it.	Do not eat it.

Past Subjunctive

The past subjunctive is formed on the stem of the preterite of the third person plural (*hablaron* — *habl-, comieron* — *com-, vivieron* — *viv-*) and the tense has two sets of endings for each conjugation. The two sets of endings have the same meaning and are interchangeable but the *-ra* form is more commonly used today. The tense is translated in many ways, depending on how it is used.

In a dependent clause the tense is often translated as might or should —. This use of should, however, is not that of duty or obligation as expressed by the verb *deber.*

Past Subjunctive

habl*ar* I might or should speak, etc.		**com***er* I might or should eat, etc.		**viv***ir* I might or should live, etc.	
habl*ara*	**habl***áramos*	**com***iera*	**com***iéramos*	**viv***iera*	**viv***iéramos*
habl*aras*	**habl***arais*	**com***ieras*	**com***ierais*	**viv***ieras*	**viv***ierais*
habl*ara*	**habl***aran*	**com***iera*	**com***ieran*	**viv***iera*	**viv***ieran*
habl*ase*	**habl***ásemos*	**com***iese*	**com***iésemos*	**viv***iese*	**viv***iésemos*
habl*ases*	**habl***aseis*	**com***ieses*	**com***ieseis*	**viv***ieses*	**viv***ieseis*
habl*ase*	**habl***asen*	**com***iese*	**com***iesen*	**viv***iese*	**viv***iesen*

Si *recibiese* **el dinero, yo pagaría la cuenta.**	If I should receive the money, I would pay the bill.
Le di el dinero para que *comprara* **el libro.**	I gave him the money in order that he might buy the book.
Temía que el médico no *llegase* **a tiempo.**	I feared that the doctor might not arrive in time.

Present Perfect Subjunctive

The present perfect subjunctive is formed with the present subjunctive of *haber* + a past participle. (may have—)

hablar, I may have spoken, you may have spoken, etc.

haya	hablado	hayamos	hablado
hayas	hablado	hayáis	hablado
haya	hablado	hayan	hablado

Temo que Juan no *haya hablado* **del asunto.**
I fear that John may not have spoken of the matter.

Past Perfect Subjunctive

The past perfect subjunctive is formed with the imperfect subjunctive of *haber* + a past participle. (might or should have—)

hablar, I might or should have spoken, etc.

hubiera	hablado	hubiéramos	hablado
hubieras	hablado	hubierais	hablado
hubiera	hablado	hubieran	hablado
hubiese	hablado	hubiésemos	hablado
hubieses	hablado	hubieseis	hablado
hubiese	hablado	hubiesen	hablado

Yo temía que Juan no *hubiera hablado* **del asunto.**
I feared that John might not have spoken of the matter.

Subjunctive Tenses

	-ar			-er, -ir	
Present	___e	___emos	___a	___amos	
	___es	___éis	___as	___áis	may___
Presente	___e	___en	___a	___an	
	___ara	___áramos	___iera	___iéramos	
	___aras	___arais	___ieras	___ierais	
Past	___ara	___aran	___iera	___ieran	might or should___
Imperfecto	___ase	___ásemos	___iese	___iésemos	
	___ases	___aseis	___ieses	___ieseis	
	___ase	___asen	___iese	___iesen	

	-ar, -er, -ir		
Present Perfect	haya___	hayamos___	may
	hayas___	hayáis___	have___
Perfecto	haya___	hayan___	

Past Perfect	hubiera___	hubiéramos___	
	hubieras___	hubierais___	might
	hubiera___	hubieran___	have___
			or
	hubiese___	hubiésemos___	should
Pluscuam-	hubieses___	hubieseis___	have___
perfecto	hubiese___	hubiesen___	

Future	-ar		-er, -ir	
Futuro	___are	___áremos ___iere	___iéremos	
seldom used;	___ares	___areis ___ieres	___iereis	may ___
replaced by	___are	___aren ___iere	___ieren	
present subj.				

Verb Synopsis of Subjunctive Tenses

hablar—yo

Subjunctive

Present	hable	I may speak
Past	hablara, hablase	I might or should speak
Present Perfect	haya hablado	I may have spoken
Past Perfect	hubiera } hablado hubiese	I might or should have spoken

Complete Verb Synopsis

hablar—él

Indicativo
Tiempos simples

Presente	habla	he speaks
Imperfecto	hablaba	he used to speak
Pretérito	habló	he spoke
Futuro	hablará	he will speak
Condicional	hablaría	he would speak

Tiempos compuestos

Perfecto	ha hablado	he has spoken
Pluscuamperfecto	había hablado	he had spoken
Pretérito perfecto	hubo hablado	he had spoken
Futuro perfecto	habrá hablado	he will have spoken
Condicional perfecto	habría hablado	he would have spoken

Subjunctivo

Presente	hable	he may speak
Imperfecto	hablara, hablase	he might or should speak
Perfecto	haya hablado	he may have spoken
Pluscuamperfecto	hubiera } hablado hubiese	he might or should have spoken

6. Uses of the Subjunctive

I. Commands, suggestions, wishes.
II. After certain verbs.
III. After impersonal expressions.
IV. After conjunctions.
V. After an indefinite antecedent.

I. Commands

1. Direct

The present subjunctive is used in direct commands, both affirmative and negative, with *usted* and *ustedes*. With *tú* and *vosotros, -as* it is used in the negative form only, the imperative being used for affirmative commands. The formation of commands is discussed in more detail in a later chapter.

Hable Ud.			**No hable Ud.**	
Hablen Uds.		Speak.	**No hablen Uds.**	Do not speak.
Habla tú.			**No hables tú.**	
Hablad vosotros			**No habléis vosotros.**	

Subject pronouns are usually omitted in commands, but, if used, they are placed after the verb.

Object pronouns follow and are attached to the verb if the command is affirmative, but precede it if negative.

Léalo (Ud.).	Read it.
No lo lea (Ud.).	Do not read it.
Escríbanlo.	Write it.
No lo escriban.	Do not write it.
Levántese.	Rise.
No se levante.	Do not rise.

2. Indirect

The third person (singular and plural) of the present subjunctive is used after *que* in an indirect command, that is, one given by means of another person (have someone do something).

The subject may precede or follow the verb, but the object pronoun must precede it, whether affirmative or negative.

Que cante María.	Have Mary sing.
Que no entre nadie.	Let nobody enter.
Que esperen.	Have them wait. Let them wait.
Que Juan *lo* escriba.	Have John write it.
Que no *lo* escriba.	Let him not write it.

The subjunctive is also used without *que* in such expressions as the following:

Cueste lo que cueste, iré.	(Let it) cost what it may, I shall go.
Venga lo que venga, estoy preparado.	(Let) come what may, I am prepared.

Suggestions

The first person plural of the present subjunctive is used to express a suggestion in which the speaker is included. Object pronouns follow and are attached to the verb if affirmative, but precede if negative.

Hablemos español.	Let us speak Spanish.
Leámos*lo*.	Let us read it.
No *lo* escribamos.	Let us not write it.

Exception: **ir** **Vamos.** Let us go.

Note: When the pronoun objects *nos, selo, sela,* etc., are joined to the verb, the final letter of the latter is dropped.

Vamos + nos = Vámonos.	Let us go away.
Leamos + se + la = Leámosela.	Let us read it to him.

Substitutes for the Subjunctive

Vamos a + an infinitive is often used instead of the subjunctive in an affirmative suggestion.

Vamos a cantar. ⎫ **Cantemos.** ⎭	Let us sing.

An infinitive, either with or without *a,* is sometimes used for a direct command.

¡Trabajar!	Work!
¡A cantar, todos!	Sing, everybody!
Traducir al inglés.	Translate to English.

Wishes

The third person (singular or plural) of the present subjunctive is used to express a wish or desire. It usually follows *que,* although the latter is sometimes omitted.

Que descanse Ud. bien.	May you rest well.
Que sean Uds. muy felices.	May you be very happy.
Que Dios se lo pague.	May God repay you.
Dios le ampare.	May God protect you.
¡Viva la República!	Long live the Republic!

¡*Ojalá!* (*que*) Oh that! Would that! I hope! Derived from the Arabic meaning "Allah grant."

The subjunctive is also used after *ojalá* to express a wish or desire. The tense varies according to the thought.

¡Ojalá que vuelvan pronto!	Oh that they return soon!
¡Ojalá sea verdad!	I hope it is true!
¡Ojalá que él estuviera aquí!	I wish that he were here!
¡Ojalá que no lo hubiera hecho!	Oh that he had not done it!

Quien, followed by the past subjunctive, may replace *ojalá* in such expressions as:

¡Quién fuera rico!	Oh that I were rich!
¡Quién lo supiera!	Oh that I knew it!

II. Subjunctive after Certain Verbs

The subjunctive is used in dependent clauses after verbs that influence it by expressing wish, desire, command, preference, approval, advice, permission, prohibition, or suggestion.

It is also used after verbs that express doubt, denial, uncertainty, and emotion.

The subjunctive is used in the dependent clause only when each clause has a different subject. If there is but one subject, an infinitive is used.

Quiero que Ud. *lea.*	I want you to read.
Quiero leer.	I want to read.
El maestro prefiere que *hablemos* español.	The teacher prefers that we speak Spanish.
Preferimos hablar inglés.	We prefer to speak English.
Siento que Ud. no lo *tenga.*	I am sorry you do not have it.
Siento no tenerlo.	I am sorry not to have it.

Sequence of Tense

The tense of the subjunctive to be used in a dependent clause is determined not only by the tense of the main verb, but also by the thought expressed. However, the following is the usual sequence.

Main Clause Verb	Dependent Clause Verb
Present Present Perfect Future Command	Present Subjunctive (Present or Present Perfect)
Imperfect Preterite Conditional Past Perfect	Past Subjunctive (Imperfect or Past Perfect)

Dudo que él esté allí.	I doubt that he is there.
Dudo que él estuviera allí.	I doubt that he was there.
Dudo que él haya estado allí.	I doubt that he has been there.
Dudaba que él estuviese allí.	I doubted that he was there.
Dudé que él hubiese ido.	I doubted that he had gone.
Digo a Juan que estudie.	I tell John to study.
Le he dicho que estudie.	I have told him to study.
Le dije que estudiase.	I told him to study.
Le había dicho que estudiase.	I had told him to study.
Le dije a Juan que lo hiciese.	I told John to do it.
Dígale Ud. a Carlos que venga.	Tell Charles to come.
Siento que Ud. no lo haya hecho.	I am sorry you have not done it.
Siento no haberlo hecho.	I am sorry not to have done it.

Quisiera

The -*ra* form of the past subjunctive of *querer* is usually used instead of the present indicative to express a wish or desire in a more polite way. While the tense is past, the thought is present.

Quiero verlo.	I want to see it.
Quisiera verlo.	I should like to see it.
Quisiera que Ud. lo viese.	I should like to have you see it.

Verbs Followed by the Subjunctive

(if there is a change of subject)

desear to desire	**proponer** to propose
querer to want	**sugerir** to suggest
***mandar** to order, to command	
decir to tell (to order)	**dudar** to doubt (positive only)
pedir to ask	**no estar seguro** not to be sure
insistir en to insist	**no creer que** not to believe
empeñarse en to insist	**no decir que** not to say
rogar to entreat	**no saber que** not to know
***hacer** to make	
preferir to prefer	**negar** to deny (positive only)
gustar to please	
aprobar to approve	**alegrarse de** to be glad
***aconsejar** to advise	**esperar** to hope
***permitir** to permit	**extrañarse** to be surprised
***dejar** to allow	**sentir** to regret
***prohibir** to prohibit	**temer** to fear
impedir to prevent	**tener miedo** to be afraid

*These verbs may be followed by either an infinitive, or the subjunctive.

Le aconsejo que estudie.	I advise him to study.
Le aconsejo estudiar.	
Le mandó que lo hiciera.	He ordered him to do it.
Le mandó hacerlo.	
Les hizo callarse.	He made them be silent.

III. Impersonal Expressions

Impersonal verbs are verbs which have no definite subject. In English they are used with an indefinite it.

Impersonal verbs are used only in the third person singular of the various tenses.

Impersonal Expressions

es necesario ⎫ es menester ⎬ it is necessary es preciso ⎭	es lástima it is a pity es triste it is sad
es importante ⎫ importa ⎬ it is important	es dudoso it is doubtful parece mentira it is hard to be- lieve
es fácil it is easy es difícil it is difficult	es hora de ⎫ es tiempo de ⎬ it is time
es posible it is possible es imposible it is impossible puede ser que it may be	más vale it is better conviene it is fitting basta it is enough
es probable it is probable es improbable it is improbable	es cierto it is certain es verdad it is true
es bueno it is good, it is well es malo it is bad	es claro ⎫ es evidente ⎬ it is evident

1. Impersonal expressions (except those expressing certainty) are followed by the subjunctive if the dependent verb has a definite subject, expressed or implied; if not, an infinitive is used.

Es necesario que Ud. *estudie.*	⎧It is necessary that you study. ⎨It is necessary for you to study.
Es necesario estudiar para aprender.	It is necessary to study in order to learn.
Fue importante que él lo *hiciese.*	⎧It was important that he do it. ⎨It was important for him to do it.
Fue importante hacerlo.	It was important to do it.

2. An infinitive may follow an impersonal verb if the latter is preceded by an indirect object pronoun.

Me es imposible ir.	It is impossible for me to go.
Le importa saberlo.	It is important for him to know it.

Expressions of Certainty
(not followed by the subjunctive)

Es evidente que él no lo *sabe.*	It is evident that he does not know it.
Es verdad que María *está* **enferma.**	It is true that Mary is ill.

Es cierto que Juan lo *hizo*.	It is certain that John did it.
But: No es cierto que *hayan llegado*.	It is not certain that they have arrived.

IV. Subjunctive after Conjunctions

As a general rule, the subjunctive is used after conjunctions of time, concession, purpose, condition, and supposition, only when the verb of the dependent clause expresses something as not yet accomplished or not yet a fact.

Conjunctions

Time
*antes de que	before
así que	
luego que	as soon as
tan pronto como	

cuando	when
después (de) que	after
hasta que	until

Concession
aunque	although
aun cuando	even if
a pesar de que	in spite of the fact

Purpose
*para que	
*a fin de que	in order that
de modo que	
de manera que	so that

Condition
*a condición de que	on condition that
*con tal que	
*a menos que	unless
si	if

Supposition
*dado que	supposing that
*suponiendo que	
*en (el) caso de que	in case

*como si	as if
*sin que	without
por + (adj. or adv.)	que + however

*Always followed by the subjunctive.

1. The subjunctive follows conjunctions of time and concession only when the verb refers to future time.

Compraré flores cuando *vaya* al mercado.	I shall buy flowers when I go to the market.
Compré flores cuando *fui* al mercado.	I bought flowers when I went to the market.
Escriba Ud. tan pronto como *llegue*.	Write as soon as you arrive.
Escribió luego que *llegó*.	He wrote as soon as he arrived.
Iré aunque *llueva*.	I shall go although it may rain.
Fui aunque *llovió*.	I went although it rained.
Lo *haré* a pesar de que *sea* difícil.	I shall do it in spite of the fact that it may be difficult.
Lo *hice* a pesar de que *fue* difícil.	I did it in spite of the fact that it was difficult.

2. Conjunctions of purpose, condition, and supposition are nearly always followed by the subjunctive. Because of its meaning, the verb in the dependent clause seldom expresses anything as having been accomplished.

Le mando a la escuela para que *aprenda.*	I send him to school in order that he may learn. (It does not say that he learns.)
Le di el dinero para que *comprara* **el libro.**	I gave him the money in order that he might buy the book. (It does not say that he bought it.)
Iré a condición de que María *vaya.*	I shall go on condition that Mary goes.
Le dije que no lo haría a menos que me *pagara.*	I told him that I would not do it unless he paid me.
Se lo daré en caso de que *venga.*	I shall give it to him in case he comes.
Yo lo llevaba en caso de que le *viera.*	I took it in case I should see him.

Infinitive Used after a Preposition

Conjunctions should not be confused with prepositions, many of which have a corresponding form. A preposition followed by an infinitive is used when there is no change of subject in the sentence.

Juan estudia para *aprender.*	John studies in order to learn.
Le ayudo para que *aprenda.*	I help him in order that he may learn.
Lo haré antes de *salir.*	I shall do it before going out.
Lo haré antes de que *vengan.*	I shall do it before they come.

Conjunctions	Prepositions	
para que	**para**	in order
sin que	**sin**	without
hasta que	**hasta**	until
después de que	**después**	after
antes de que	**antes de**	before
cuando	**al**	when, on

3. Si—if

The past subjunctive, simple or compound, is used after the conjunction *si,* if the clause which follows expresses a condition contrary to fact, or if it refers to something doubtful of fulfillment in the future.

It is well to remember that, if the result clause is expressed in English with would or would have, the past subjunctive is always used in the if clause in Spanish.

Either form of the past subjunctive may be used in the if clause. The result clause is generally expressed with the conditional, but the -ra form of the subjunctive may also be used.

Si Pedro *estudiara, aprendería.* **(or aprendiera)**	If Peter studied, he would learn. (The fact is he does not study.)
Si yo *tuviera* **tiempo, lo** *haría.*	If I had time I would do it.

Si *recibiese* el dinero, *pagaría* la cuenta.	If I should receive the money, I would pay the bill.
Si yo *hubiera recibido* el dinero, la *habría pagado.*	If I had received the money, I would have paid it.
¿Iría Ud. al campo si *lloviese?*	Would you go to the country if it should rain?

A gerund can be used as a substitute for an if clause.

Teniendo tiempo, yo lo haría.	If I had time, I would do it.
Habiendo tenido tiempo, lo habría hecho.	If I had had time, I would have done it.

Many if clauses do not require a subjunctive.

Si *llueve* mañana, no *iremos* a la playa.	If it rains tomorrow, we shall not go to the beach.
Si *llovía,* no *íbamos* a la escuela.	If it rained, we did not go to school.
Si él *ha escrito, contéstele.*	If he has written, answer him.
Si él le *escribió* a Ud., ¿por qué no le *contestó?*	If he wrote to you, why did you not answer him?

Como si, as if, is always followed by the past subjunctive.

Margarita habla como si *fuera* española.	Margaret speaks as if she were Spanish.
Siguió como si no *hubiera oído* nada.	He continued as if he had heard nothing.

Sin que, without, is always followed by the subjunctive (pres. or past).

Rosa lo hace sin que su madre lo *sepa.*	Rose does it without her mother's knowing it.
Rosa lo hizo sin que su madre lo *supiera.*	Rose did it without her mother's knowing it.

Por + (adj. or adv.) + *que,* however, is followed by the subjunctive if uncertainty is implied.

Por rica que *sea,* no la envidio.	However rich she may be, I do not envy her.
Por rápidamente que *corra,* no llegará Ud. a tiempo.	However fast you may run, you will not arrive in time.

V. Subjunctive after an Indefinite Antecedent

A relative is a connecting word that refers to something previously mentioned in the sentence.

The subjunctive is used after a relative that refers to something unknown, not definitely known, or nonexistent, called the indefinite antecedent.

Necesito *un libro que tenga* **mapas.**   I need a book that has maps.
Un libro is the indefinite antecedent of the relative *que.*

Necesito *el libro* **que** *tiene* **mapas.**	I need the book that has maps.

El libro is the definite antecedent and, therefore, no subjunctive is used.

Busco *una criada* **que** *hable* **español.**	I am looking for a maid who speaks Spanish.
Necesitaban *una criada* **que** *hablase* **español.**	They needed a maid who spoke Spanish.
No hay *hombre* **que** *quiera* **hacer eso.**	There is no man who wants to do that.

Words often used as indefinite antecedents

algo	something	**los que, las que**	those who
nada	nothing	**el que, la que**	the one who
alguien	some one, any one	**cuandoquiera**	whenever
nadie	nobody, any one	**dondequiera**	wherever
alguno, (-a, -os, -as)	any, some	**cualquier, -a**	whichever
ninguno, -a	no one, none	**quienquiera**	whoever

lo que   what, whatever

Quiero algo que sea útil.	I want something that is useful.
No veo nada que me guste.	I do not see anything that I like.
¿Hay alguien que lo sepa?	Is there any one who knows it?
No hay nadie que lo sepa.	There is no one who knows it.
Necesitan algunos obreros que hablen español.	They need some workmen who speak Spanish.
No hay ninguno que hable español.	There is no one who speaks Spanish.
El que lo haga primero recibirá el dinero.	The one who does it first will receive the money.
Iré cuandoquiera que Ud. me diga.	I shall go whenever you tell me.
Iré adondequiera que él vaya.	I shall go wherever he goes.
Quienquiera que sea, la ayudaré.	Whoever she may be, I shall help her.
Tome Ud. cualquier libro que le guste.	Take whichever book you like.
Haré lo que Ud. quiera.	I shall do whatever you wish.

7. Progressive Tenses

The progressive tenses indicate an action as unfinished and as continuing. The progressive forms of all tenses are formed by using the different tenses of *estar* with a gerund, that is, the form of the verb ending in -ing.

A gerund is formed by adding *-ando* to the stem of *-ar* verbs and *-iendo* to *-er* and *-ir* verbs.

habl*ar*,	habl*ando*,	speaking
com*er*,	com*iendo*,	eating
viv*ir*,	viv*iendo*,	living

Present Progressive
hablar

I am speaking, you are speaking, he is speaking, etc.

estoy	hablando	estamos	hablando
estás	hablando	estáis	hablando
está	hablando	están	hablando

Juan *está hablando.*	John is talking.
¿**Qué** *está Ud. comiendo?*	What are you eating?
Estaban cantándola.	They were singing it.
La *estaban cantando.*	They were singing it.
Estoy escribiendo.	I am writing.
¿**A quién** *está Ud. escribiendo?*	To whom are you writing?

Verb Synopsis in the Progressive Tenses

hablar—yo

Indicative		
Present	**estoy hablando**	I am speaking
Imperfect	**estaba hablando**	I was speaking
Preterite	**estuve hablando**	I was speaking
Future	**estaré hablando**	I shall be speaking
Conditional	**estaría hablando**	I would be speaking
Present Perfect	**he estado hablando**	I have been speaking
Past Perfect	**había estado hablando**	I had been speaking
Pret. Perfect	**hube estado hablando**	I had been speaking
Future Perfect	**habré estado hablando**	I shall have been speaking

Cond. Perfect	**habría estado hablando**	I would have been speaking

Subjunctive

Present	**esté hablando**	I may be speaking
Past	**estuviera**⎫ **hablando** **estuviese**⎭	I might or should be speaking
Present Perfect	**haya estado hablando**	I may have been speaking
Past Perfect	**hubiera**⎫ **estado** **hubiese**⎭ **hablando**	I might or should have been speaking

Ir, venir, and *ser* are never used in the progressive form.

Ir, to go, and *venir,* to come, are often used with a gerund.

Van **cantando por la calle.**	They go singing through the street.
El *viene* **corriendo.**	He comes running.

Seguir and *continuar,* to continue, are used with a gerund instead of an infinitive.

El *sigue* **hablando.**	He continues talking. He continues to talk.
Continuó **gritando.**	He continued to shout. He kept on shouting.

8. Irregular Verbs

Only the irregular tenses are given; the remaining tenses of the verbs are regular.

The present subjunctive is usually formed on the stem of the first person singular of the present indicative, and the past subjunctive is always formed on the stem of the preterite, third person plural. The familiar affirmative command (*habla tú*) is usually like the third person singular of the present indicative.

andar   to walk   *andando*   *andado*

Pret. **anduve, anduviste, anduvo, anduvimos, anduvisteis, anduvieron**
Past Subj. **anduviera, anduvieras, anduviera, anduviéramos, anduvierais, anduvieran**

asir   to seize   *asiendo*   *asido*

Pres. **asgo,** ases, ase, asimos, asís, asen
Pres. Subj. **asga, asgas, asga, asgamos, asgáis, asgan**

caber   to be contained in *cabiendo*   *cabido*

Pres. **quepo,** cabes, cabe, cabemos, cabéis, caben
Pret. **cupe, cupiste, cupo, cupimos, cupisteis, cupieron**
Fut. **cabré, cabrás, cabrá, cabremos, cabréis, cabrán**
Cond. **cabría, cabrías, cabría, cabríamos, cabríais, cabrían**
Pres. Subj. **quepa, quepas, quepa, quepamos, quepáis, quepan**
Past Subj. **cupiera, cupieras, cupiera, cupiéramos, cupierais, cupieran**

caer   to fall   *cayendo*   *caído*

Pres. **caigo,** caes, cae, caemos, caéis, caen
Pret. caí, **caíste, cayó, caímos, caísteis, cayeron**
Pres. Subj. **caiga, caigas, caiga, caigamos, caigáis, caigan**
Past Subj. **cayera, cayeras, cayera, cayéramos, cayerais, cayeran**

*Note: When the endings *-iste, -isteis, -imos, -ido* follow a strong vowel (*a, e, o*) the first i of the ending has a written accent, which is needed to break the diphthong. (ca*í*ste)

If these endings follow the weak vowel *u*, they form a diphthong composed of two weak vowels, in which case the second one is stressed and does not need a written accent.

dar to give   *dando*   *dado*

Pres. **doy,** das, da, damos, dais, dan
Pret. **di, diste, dio,** dimos, disteis, **dieron**
Pres. Subj. **dé,** des, **dé,** demos, deis, **den**
Past Subj. **diera, dieras, diera, diéramos, dierais, dieran**

decir to say; to tell   *diciendo*   *dicho*

Pres. **digo, dices, dice,** decimos, decís, **dicen**
Pret. **dije, dijiste, dijo, dijimos, dijisteis, dijeron**
Fut. **diré, dirás, dirá, diremos, diréis, dirán**
Cond. **diría, dirías, diría, diríamos, diríais, dirían**
Pres. Subj. **diga, digas, diga, digamos, digáis, digan**
Past Subj. **dijera, dijeras, dijera, dijéramos, dijerais, dijeran**
Imperative **di,** decid

estar to be   *estando*   *estado*

Pres. **estoy, estás, está,** estamos, estáis, **están**
Pret. **estuve, estuviste, estuvo, estuvimos, estuvisteis, estuvieron**
Pres. Subj. **esté, estés, esté,** estemos, estéis, **estén**
Past Subj. **estuviera, estuvieras, estuviera, estuviéramos, estuvierais, estuvieran**
Imperative **está,** estad

haber to have   *habiendo*   *habido*

Pres. **he, has, ha, hemos,** habéis, **han**
Pret. **hube, hubiste, hubo, hubimos, hubisteis, hubieron**
Fut. **habré, habrás, habrá, habremos, habréis, habrán**
Cond. **habría, habrías, habría, habríamos, habríais, habrían**
Pres. Subj. **haya, hayas, haya, hayamos, hayáis, hayan**
Past Subj. **hubiera, hubieras, hubiera, hubiéramos, hubierais, hubieran**
Imperative **he,** habed

hacer to do; to make   *haciendo*   *hecho*

Pres. **hago,** haces, hace, hacemos, hacéis, hacen
Pret. **hice, hiciste, hizo, hicimos, hicisteis, hicieron**
Fut. **haré, harás, hará, haremos, haréis, harán**
Cond. **haría, harías, haría, haríamos, haríais, harían**
Pres. Subj. **haga, hagas, haga, hagamos, hagáis, hagan**
Past Subj. **hiciera, hicieras, hiciera, hiciéramos, hicierais, hicieran**
Imperative **haz,** haced

ir to go   *yendo*   *ido*

Pres. **voy, vas, va, vamos, vais, van**
Imper. **iba, ibas, iba, íbamos, ibais, iban**
Pret. **fui, fuiste, fue, fuimos, fuisteis, fueron**
Pres. Subj. **vaya, vayas, vaya, vayamos, vayáis, vayan**
Past Subj. **fuera, fueras, fuera, fuéramos, fuerais, fueran**
Imperative **ve,** id

oír to hear *oyendo* *oído*

Pres. **oigo, oyes, oye, oímos, oís, oyen**
Pret. **oí, oíste, oyó, oímos, oísteis, oyeron**
Pres. Subj. **oiga, oigas, oiga, oigamos, oigáis, oigan**
Past Subj. **oyera, oyeras, oyera, oyéramos, oyerais, oyeran**
Imperative **oye,** oíd

oler to smell *oliendo* *olido*

Pres. **huelo, hueles, huele,** olemos, oléis, **huelen**
Pres. Subj. **huela, huelas, huela,** olamos, oláis, **huelan**
Imperative **huele,** oled

poder to be able *pudiendo* *podido*

Pres. **puedo, puedes, puede,** podemos, podéis, **pueden**
Pret. **pude, pudiste, pudo, pudimos, pudisteis, pudieron**
Fut. **podré, podrás, podrá, podremos, podréis, podrán**
Cond. **podría, podrías, podría, podríamos, podríais, podrían**
Pres. Subj. **pueda, puedas, pueda,** podamos, podáis, **puedan**
Past Subj. **pudiera, pudieras, pudiera, pudiéramos, pudierais, pudieran**

poner to put; to place *poniendo* *puesto*

Pres. **pongo,** pones, pone, ponemos, ponéis, ponen
Pret. **puse, pusiste, puso, pusimos, pusisteis, pusieron**
Fut. **pondré, pondrás, pondrá, pondremos, pondréis, pondrán**
Cond. **pondría, pondrías, pondría, pondríamos, pondríais, pondrían**
Pres. Subj. **ponga, pongas, ponga, pongamos, pongáis, pongan**
Past Subj. **pusiera, pusieras, pusiera, pusiéramos, pusierais, pusieran**
Imperative **pon,** poned

querer to wish; to want *queriendo* *querido*

Pres. **quiero, quieres, quiere,** queremos, queréis, **quieren**
Pret. **quise, quisiste, quiso, quisimos, quisisteis, quisieron**
Fut. **querré, querrás, querrá, querremos, querréis, querrán**
Cond. **querría, querrías, querría, querríamos, querríais, querrían**
Pres. Subj. **quiera, quieras, quiera,** queramos, queráis, **quieran**
Past Subj. **quisiera, quisieras, quisiera, quisiéramos, quisierais, quisieran**

saber to know *sabiendo* *sabido*

Pres. **sé,** sabes, sabe, sabemos, sabéis, saben
Pret. **supe, supiste, supo, supimos, supisteis, supieron**
Fut. **sabré, sabrás, sabrá, sabremos, sabréis, sabrán**
Cond. **sabría, sabrías, sabría, sabríamos, sabríais, sabrían**
Pres. Subj. **sepa, sepas, sepa, sepamos, sepáis, sepan**
Past Subj. **supiera, supieras, supiera, supiéramos, supierais, supieran**

salir   to go out   *saliendo*   *salido*

Pres. **salgo,** sales, sale, salimos, salís, salen
Fut. **saldré, saldrás, saldrá, saldremos, saldréis, saldrán**
Cond. **saldría, saldrías, saldría, saldríamos, saldríais, saldrían**
Pres. Subj. **salga, salgas, salga, salgamos, salgáis, salgan**
Imperative **sal,** salid

ser   to be   . *siendo*   *sido*

Pres. **soy, eres, es, somos, sois, son**
Imp. **era, eras, era, éramos, erais, eran**
Pret. **fui, fuiste, fue, fuimos, fuisteis, fueron**
Pres. Subj. **sea, seas, sea, seamos, seáis, sean**
Past Subj. **fuera, fueras, fuera, fuéramos, fuerais, fueran**
Imperative **sé,** sed

tener   to have   *teniendo*   *tenido*

Pres. **tengo, tienes, tiene,** tenemos, tenéis, **tienen**
Pret. **tuve, tuviste, tuvo, tuvimos, tuvisteis, tuvieron**
Fut. **tendré, tendrás, tendrá, tendremos, tendréis, tendrán**
Cond. **tendría, tendrías, tendría, tendríamos, tendríais, tendrían**
Pres. Subj. **tenga, tengas, tenga, tengamos, tengáis, tengan**
Past Subj. **tuviera, tuvieras, tuviera, tuviéramos, tuvierais, tuvieran**
Imperative **ten,** tened

traer   to bring   *trayendo*   *traído*

Pres. **traigo,** traes, trae, traemos, traéis, traen
Pret. **traje, trajiste, trajo, trajimos, trajisteis, trajeron**
Pres. Subj. **traigo, traigas, traiga, traigamos, traigáis, traigan**
Past Subj. **trajera, trajeras, trajera, trajéramos, trajerais, trajeran**

valer   to be worth   *valiendo*   *valido*

Pres. **valgo,** vales, vale, valemos, valéis, valen
Fut. **valdré, valdrás, valdrá, valdremos, valdréis, valdrán**
Cond. **valdría, valdrías, valdría, valdríamos, valdríais, valdrían**
Pres. Subj. **valga, valgas, valga, valgamos, valgáis, valgan**
Imperative **val,** valed

venir   to come   *viniendo*   *venido*

Pres. **vengo, vienes, viene,** venimos, venís, **vienen**
Pret. **vine, viniste, vino, vinimos, vinisteis, vinieron**
Fut. **vendré, vendrás, vendrá, vendremos, vendréis, vendrán**
Cond. **vendría, vendrías, vendría, vendríamos, vendríais, vendrían**
Pres. Subj. **venga, vengas, venga, vengamos, vengáis, vengan**
Past Subj. **viniera, vinieras, viniera, viniéramos, vinierais, vinieran**
Imperative **ven,** venid

ver   to see   *viendo*   *visto*

Pres. **veo,** ves, ve, vemos, veis, ven
Imp. **veía, veías, veía, veíamos, veíais, veían**
Pres. Subj. **vea, veas, vea, veamos, veáis, vean**

Other Irregular Verbs

Other irregular verbs are grouped according to a similarity of endings and spelling changes.

- zar   vowel⟩ - cer   - ducir   - eer   - uir   - llir   - iar
                     - cir   - güir   - ñer   - uar
                                                        - ñir

-zar

Although the sound remains the same, the following change is required: Change *z* to *c* before *e*. (crucé)

cruzar   to cross   *cruzando*   *cruzado*

Pret. **crucé,** cruzaste, cruzó, cruzamos, cruzasteis, cruzaron
Pres. Subj. **cruce, cruces, cruce, crucemos, crucéis, crucen**
Other verbs of this type are:

abrazar to embrace	**cruzar** to cross
alzar to raise	**empezar(ie)** to begin
alcanzar to reach	**gozar** to enjoy
aplazar to postpone	**lanzar** to cast
cazar to hunt	**organizar** to organize
comenzar(ie) to begin	**rezar** to pray

-cer, -cir preceded by a vowel

Insert *z* before the endings *-co, -ca* (cono**z**co)

conocer   to be acquainted with, know *conociendo*   *conocido*

Pres. **conozco,** conoces, conoce, conocemos, conocéis, conocen
Pres. Subj. **conozca, conozcas, conozca, conozcamos, conozcáis, conozcan**

Exceptions: *cocer (ue),* to cook, and *mecer,* to rock, do not add *z* but change *c* to *z* before *-o, -a.*

Other verbs of this type are:

aborrecer to hate	**establecer** to establish
agradecer to thank, to be grateful	**merecer** to merit, deserve
aparecer to appear	**obedecer** to obey
desaparecer to disappear	**desobedecer** to disobey
compadecer to pity	**ofrecer** to offer
conocer to know	**padecer** to suffer
reconocer to recognize	**permanecer** to remain
crecer to grow	**pertenecer** to belong to

-ducir

Insert *z* before *-co, -ca* (tradu**zco**)

These verbs are also irregular in the preterite and the past subjunctive.

traducir   to translate   *traduciendo*   *traducido*

Pres. **traduzco,** traduces, traduce, traducimos, traducís, traducen
Pret. **traduje, tradujiste, tradujo, tradujimos, tradujisteis, tradujeron**
Pres. Subj. **traduzca, traduzcas, traduzca, traduzcamos, traduzcáis, traduzcan**
Past Subj. **tradujera, tradujeras, tradujera, tradujéramos, tradujerais, tradujeran**

Other verbs of this type are:

conducir to conduct	**introducir** to introduce
deducir to deduce	**producir** to produce
inducir to induce	**reducir** to reduce

-eer

Add a written accent to the *i* in all the stressed syllables. (leíste)
Change the unaccented *i* to *y* between vowels. (leyeron)

leer   to read   *leyendo*   *leído*

Pret. leí, **leíste, leyó, leímos, leísteis, leyeron**
Past Subj. **leyera, leyeras, leyera, leyéramos, leyerais, leyeran**

Other verbs of this type are:

creer to believe	**proveer** to provide
poseer to possess	

-uir, -güir

Insert *y* before *a, e, o* and also change the unaccented *i* to *y* between vowels. (huyó)

huir   to flee   *huyendo*   *huido*

Pres. **huyo, huyes, huye,** huimos, huis, **huyen**
Pret. huí, huiste, **huyó,** huimos, huisteis, **huyeron**
Pres. Subj. **huya, huyas, huya, huyamos, huyáis, huyan**
Past Subj. **huyera, huyeras, huyera, huyéramos, huyerais, huyeran**
Imperative **huye,** huid
Gerund **huyendo**

Other verbs of this type are:

atribuir to attribute	**excluir** to exclude
constituir to constitute	**huir** to flee
construir to construct	**incluir** to include
destruir to destroy	**instruir** to instruct
distribuir to distribute	**concluir** to conclude

-*güir*

The dieresis is retained only before an *i;* other changes are like -*uir* verbs.

argüir   to argue   *arguyendo*   *argüido*

Pres. **arguyo, arguyes, arguye, argüimos, argüís, arguyen**
Imperf. **argüía, argüías,** etc.
Pret. **argüí, argüiste, arguyó, argüimos, argüisteis, arguyeron**
Fut. **argüiré,** etc.
Cond. **argüiría,** etc.
Pres. Subj. **arguya, arguyas, arguya, arguyamos, arguyáis, arguyan**
Past Subj. **arguyera,** etc.
Imperative **arguye, argüid**

-*llir, -ñer, -ñir*

Drop the *i* of the endings -*ió* and -*ie* when they follow *ll* and *ñ*.

gruñir   to growl   *gruñendo*   *gruñido*

Pret. **gruñí,** gruñiste, **gruñó,** gruñimos, gruñisteis, **gruñeron**
Past Subj. **gruñera, gruñeras, gruñera, gruñéramos, gruñerais, gruñeran**
Gerund **gruñendo**

Other verbs of this type are:

bullir to boil	**bruñir** to burnish, polish
zambullir to dive	**ceñir** (i) to gird
tañer to twang	**reñir** (i) to quarrel, scold
	teñir (i) to dye

-*iar, -uar*

Some verbs ending in -*iar* and -*uar* require a written accent to the *i* or *u* of certain syllables in order to preserve the correct sound of the word (usually learned by practice).

Add a written accent to the last vowel of the stem before all unaccented or unstressed endings.

enviar   to send   *enviando*   *enviado*

Pres. **envío, envías, envía,** enviamos, enviáis, **envían**
Pres. Subj. **envíe, envíes, envíe,** enviemos, enviéis, **envíen**
Imp. **envía, enviad**

continuar   to continue   *continuando*   *continuado*

Pres. **continúo, continúas, continúa,** continuamos, continuáis, **continúan**
Pres. Subj. **continúe, continúes, continúe,** continuemos, continuéis, **continúen**
Imperative **continúa, continuad**

Other verbs of this type are:

ataviar to adorn	**acentuar** to accent
confiar to trust	**continuar** to continue

criar   to raise, rear
enfriar   to cool
enviar   to send
espiar   to spy
guiar   to guide
liar   to bind
telegrafiar   to telegraph
vaciar   to empty
variar   to vary

efectuar   to accomplish
evacuar   to evacuate
exceptuar   to except
fluctuar   to fluctuate
graduar   to graduate
insinuar   to insinuate
perpetuar   to perpetuate
puntuar   to punctuate

The following verbs are exceptions to the above and are conjugated regularly.

anunciar   to announce
apreciar   to appreciate
asociar   to associate
cambiar   to change
envidiar   to envy
estudiar   to study

iniciar   to initiate
limpiar   to clean
odiar   to hate
principiar   to begin
pronunciar   to pronounce
renunciar   to renounce

9. *Estar, Ser*

Although there are many other uses for these verbs, it is well to remember that *ser* tells what anything is, and *estar* tells where it is. The conjugations of these verbs are irregular in many of the tenses. Please refer to the chapter on irregular verbs for their conjugations.

Madrid *es* **una ciudad.**	Madrid is a city.
Madrid *está* **en España.**	Madrid is in Spain.

Estar

1. To express location or position

El libro *está* **en la mesa.**	The book is on the table.
Juan *está* **en el campo.**	John is in the country.

2. To express a temporary or variable condition or state

Juan *está* **enfermo.**	John is sick.
La ventana *está* **abierta.**	The window is open.

3. To express a state of health

Juan *está* **bien.**	John is well.
María *está* **mala.**	Mary is ill.

4. To form the progressive tenses

Juan *está* **estudiando.**	John is studying.

Ser

1. To identify a person or an object

El edificio *es* **un templo.**	The building is a temple.
Es **Juan.** *Es* **ella.**	It is John. It is she.

2. To express inherent qualities or characteristics (appearances, character, size, color, material, state of being)

María *es* **bonita.**	Mary is pretty.
María *es* **buena.**	Mary is good.
La casa *es* **grande.**	The house is large.
La casa *es* **blanca.**	The house is white.

Su traje *es* de seda.	Her dress is of silk.
Juan *es* rico.	John is rich.
Carlos *es* pobre.	Charles is poor.
María *es* joven.	Mary is young.
Su abuela *es* vieja.	Her grandmother is old.

3. To express nationality, occupation, origin

ˋJuan *es* español.	John is Spanish.
Es carpintero.	He is a carpenter.
Juan *es* de España.	John is from Spain.

4. To tell time

¿Qué hora *es?*	What time is it?
Son las tres.	It's three o'clock.

5. To express ownership

Los libros *son* de Juan.	The books are John's.

6. In impersonal expressions

Es necesario.	It is necessary.
Es posible.	It is possible.

7. To express the passive voice (used with a past participle)

El teléfono *fue* inventado por Bell.	The telephone was invented by Bell.
Las islas *fueron* descubiertas por Colón.	The islands were discovered by Columbus.

10. Radical-Changing Verbs

These verbs change the vowel of the stem in certain parts of certain tenses. If there is more than one vowel in the stem, the one nearest the end is changed. The verbs are grouped into three classes according to the endings and changes. *-Ar* and *-er* verbs belong to the first class. *-Ir* verbs belong to either the second or third class, according to how they change.

Class I

-ar, -er verbs

o changes to *ue*   *e* changes to *ie*

The change to *ue* or *ie* always occurs in the stressed syllable of the verb. Changes occur in three tenses only.

contar to count   *contando*   *contado*

Present

1. c*ue*nto	1. contamos
2. c*ue*ntas	2. contáis
3. c*ue*nta	3. c*ue*ntan

Present Subjunctive

1. c*ue*nte	1. contemos
2. c*ue*ntes	2. contéis
3. c*ue*nte	3. c*ue*nten

Imperative

c*ue*nta   contad

Sample Verbs of the First Class

almorzar to lunch	**sentar(se)** to seat; to sit
apostar to wager	**disolver** to dissolve
contar to count	**mover** to move
despertar(se) to awake	**oler**[2] to smell
errar[1] to err	**perder** to lose
jugar to play	**resolver** to resolve
pensar to think	**volver** to return

[1]Whenever a verb form begins with *ie*, it is written *ye*.
[2]When a verb form begins with *ue*, it is written *hue*.

errar to err, make a mistake

Pres. **yerro, yerras, yerra,** erramos, erráis, **yerran**
Pres. Subj. **yerre, yerres, yerre,** erremos, erréis, **yerren**
Imperative **yerra,** errad

oler to smell

Pres. **huelo, hueles, huele,** olemos, oléis, **huelen**
Pres. Subj. **huela, huelas, huela,** olamos, oláis, **huelan**
Imperative **huele,** oled

Class II

-ir verbs

o changes to *ue* and also to *u*
e changes to *ie* and also to *i*

Changes occur in five tenses and the gerund.

dormir to sleep   *durmiendo*   *dormido*

Present

1. d*u*ermo
2. d*u*ermes
3. d*u*erme

1. dormimos
2. dormís
3. d*u*ermen

Preterite

1. dormí
2. dormiste
3. d*u*rmió

1. dormimos
2. dormisteis
3. d*u*rmieron

Present Subjunctive

1. d*u*erma
2. d*u*ermas
3. d*u*erma

1. d*u*rmamos
2. d*u*rmáis
3. d*u*erman

Past Subjunctive

1. d*u*rmiera
2. d*u*rmieras
3. d*u*rmiera

1. d*u*rmiéramos
2. d*u*rmierais
3. d*u*rmieran

Imperative
d*u*erme   dormid

Gerund
d*u*rmiendo

Sample Verbs of the Second Class

advertir to warn	**mentir** to lie
consentir to consent	**morir** to die
convertir to convert	**preferir** to prefer

divertir(se)	to amuse (oneself)	**referir**	to refer
dormir(se)	to sleep; to fall asleep	**sentir**	to feel; regret

Class III

-ir verbs

e changes to *i*

Changes occur in five tenses and the gerund.

vestir   to dress   *vistiendo*   *vestido*

Present

1. v*i*sto	1. **vestimos**
2. v*i*stes	2. **vestís**
3. v*i*ste	3. v*i*sten

Preterite

1. **vestí**	1. **vestimos**
2. **vestiste**	2. **vestisteis**
3. v*i*stió	3. v*i*stieron

Present Subjunctive

1. v*i*sta	1. v*i*stamos
2. v*i*stas	2. v*i*stáis
3. v*i*sta	3. v*i*stan

Past Subjunctive

1. v*i*stiera	1. v*i*stiéramos
2. v*i*stieras	2. v*i*stierais
3. v*i*stiera	3. v*i*stieran

Imperative

v*i*ste   **vestid**

Gerund

v*i*stiendo

Sample Verbs of the Third Class

competir	to compete	**pedir**	to ask
corregir	to correct	**reír**[1]**(se)**	to laugh
despedir(se)	to take leave of	**reñir**	to scold, to quarrel
elegir	to elect	**repetir**	to repeat
freír[1]	to fry	**sonreír**[1]	to smile
impedir	to prevent	**servir**	to serve
medir	to measure	**vestir(se)**	to dress

[1] In addition to the regular accents, verbs ending in **-eir** have a written accent over the i in all stressed syllables. They also drop one i when double i occurs.

Table of Radical Changes

Each dash represents a vowel change

	Class I -ar, -er o > ue e > ie		Class II -ir o > ue, u e > ie, i		Class III -ir e > i	
Present	1 __	1	1 __	1	1 _	1
	2 __	2	2 __	2	2 _	2
	3 __	3 __	3 __	3 __	3 _	3 _
Preterite			1	1	1	1
			2	2	2	2
			3 _	3 _	3 _	3 _
Present Subjunctive	1 __	1	1 __	1 _	1 _	1 _
	2 __	2	2 __	2 _	2 _	2 _
	3 __	3 __	3 __	3 __	3 _	3 _
Past Subjunctive			1 _	1 _	1 _	1 _
			2 _	2 _	2 _	2 _
			3 _	3 _	3 _	3 _
Imperative	__		__		_	
Gerund			_		_	

11. Orthographic-Changing Verbs

Classified as orthographic-changing verbs are those that change the spelling in order to preserve the sound of the last consonant of the stem. These verbs may be grouped according to a similarity of endings and changes.

-car -gar	consonant >	-cer -cir	-ger -gir	-guir -quir	-guar

-car

Change the *c* to *qu* before *e*.

sacar   to take out   *sacando*   *sacado*

Pret. **saqué,** sacaste, sacó, sacamos, sacasteis, sacaron
Pres. Subj. **saque, saques, saque, saquemos, saquéis, saquen**

Other verbs of this type are:

acercarse   to approach
brincar   to leap, jump
colocar   to place
educar   to educate
embarcar   to embark
explicar   to explain
fabricar   to manufacture
indicar   to indicate

marcar   to mark
mascar   to chew
publicar   to publish
rascar   to scrape; to scratch
sacar   to take out
secar   to dry
significar   to mean; to signify
tocar   to touch; to play a musical instrument

-gar

Change the *g* to *gu* before *e*.

pagar   to pay   *pagando*   *pagado*

Pret. **pagué,** pagaste, pagó, pagamos, pagasteis, pagaron
Pres. Subj. **pague, pagues, pague, paguemos, paguéis, paguen**

Other verbs of this type are:

apagar   to extinguish
castigar   to punish
colgar(ue)   to hang
entregar   to hand over; to give
investigar   to investigate

llegar   to arrive
navegar   to navigate
obligar   to compel
pegar   to beat; to stick
regar(ie)   to irrigate

-cer, -cir preceded by a consonant

Change the *c* to *z* before *o* and *a*.

vencer   to conquer   *venciendo*   *vencido*

Pres. **venzo**, vences, vence, vencemos, vencéis, vencen
Pres. Subj. **venza, venzas, venza, venzamos, venzáis, venzan**

Other verbs of this type are:

convencer to convince	**esparcir** to scatter
ejercer to excercise	**fruncir** to frown
torcer(ue) to twist	**zurcir** to mend; darn

-ger, -gir

Change the *g* to *j* before *o* and *a*.

coger   to catch   *cogiendo*   *cogido*

Pres. **cojo,** coges, coge, cogemos, cogéis, cogen
Pres. Subj. **coja, cojas, coja, cojamos, cojáis, cojan**

Other verbs of this type are:

coger to catch	**corregir(i)** to correct
encoger to shrink	**dirigir** to direct
escoger to choose	**erigir** to erect
recoger to collect; gather	**exigir** to demand
proteger to protect	**fingir** to pretend
afligir to afflict	**rugir** to roar

-guir, -quir

Drop the *u* before *o* and *a* (or change the *gu* to *g* before *o* and *a*).

distinguir   to distinguish

Pres. **distingo**, distingues, distingue, distinguimos, distinguís, distinguen
Pres. Subj. **distinga, distingas, distinga, distingamos, distingáis, distingan**

Other verbs of this type are:

conseguir(i) to obtain	
distinguir to distinguish	**perseguir(i)** to pursue
extinguir to extinguish	**seguir(i)** to continue; to follow

-quir

Change the *qu* to *c* before *o* and *a*.

delinquir   to transgress

Pres. **delinco**, delinques, delinque, delinquimos, delinquís, delinquen
Pres. Subj. **delinca, delincas, delinca, delincamos, delincáis, delincan**

-guar

Add the dieresis to the *u* before *e* (or change *g to gü* before *e*).

averiguar to ascertain *averiguando* *averiguado*

Pret. **averigüé,** averiguaste, averiguó, averiguamos, averiguasteis, averiguaron

Pres. Subj. **averigüe, averigües, averigüe, averigüemos, averigüéis, averigüen**

Other verbs of this type are:

averiguar	to ascertain	**fraguar**	to forge
desaguar	to empty; drain	**santiguar**	to bless

12. Commands (Imperatives)

I. Familiar (tú, vosotros)

The singular familiar (*tú*) affirmative command, with the exception of a few irregular verbs, is formed like the third person singular of the present indicative. Regular -ar verbs end in -a, and -er and -ir verbs end in -e. The plural, without exception, is formed by changing the final -r of the infinitive to -d. The present subjunctive must be used for all negative familiar commands (second person singular and plural).

Affirmative Familiar Commands

hablar		comer	
Habla (tú)	} Speak	Come (tú)	} Eat
Hablad (vosotros)		Comed (vosotros)	

vivir	
Vive (tú)	} Live
Vivid (vosotros)	

Negative Familiar Commands

hablar		comer	
No hables (tú)	} Don't speak.	No comas (tú)	} Don't eat.
No habléis (vosotros)		No comáis (vosotros)	

vivir	
No vivas (tú)	} Don't live.
No viváis (vosotros)	

Irregular Familiar Commands

		Singular	Plural
decir	to say, to tell	di	decid
hacer	to do, to make	haz	haced
ir	to go	ve	id
irse	to go away	vete	idos
poner	to put, to place	pon	poned

salir	to go out, to leave	sal	salid
ser	to be	sé	sed
tener	to have	ten	tened
venir	to come	ven	venid

Compra el libro.	Buy the book.
No compres la pluma.	Do not buy the pen.
Bebe la leche.	Drink the milk.
No bebas el café.	Do not drink the coffee.
Escríbela mañana.	Write it tomorrow.
No la escribas hoy.	Do not write it today.
Dime la verdad.	Tell me the truth.
No me digas eso.	Do not tell me that.
Hazlo hoy.	Do it today.
No lo hagas mañana.	Do not do it tomorrow.
Ve con tu hermano.	Go with your brother.
No vayas con Roberto.	Do not go with Robert.
Vete.	Go away.
No te vayas.	Do not go away.
Ponlo en la mesa.	Put it on the table.
No lo pongas en la silla.	Do not put it on the chair.
Ponedlos aquí.	Put them here.
No los pongáis allí.	Do not put them there.
Salid temprano.	Leave early.
No salgáis tarde.	Do not leave late.
Sé bueno.	Be good.
No seas malo.	Do not be bad.
Ten paciencia.	Have patience.
No tengas miedo.	Do not be afraid.
Ven el lunes.	Come on Monday.
No vengas el viernes.	Do not come Friday.
Venid todos.	All come.
No vengáis.	Do not come.

Position of Pronouns

The subject pronoun, if used, is placed after the verb. The object pronoun follows and is attached to the command if affirmative, but the pronoun precedes if the command is negative. When pronouns are attached, it is necessary to add an accent to preserve the original stress of the verb.

Come (tú) la fruta.   **Cóme*la* (tú).**   **No *la* comas (tú).**

II. Formal *(usted, ustedes)*

The formal commands, singular and plural, use the third persons of the present subjunctive. To form the negative, just place *no* before the verb. Subject pronouns, if used, follow the command. Object pronouns follow and are attached to the affirmative commands; they precede the negatives.

Affirmative Formal Commands

hablar
Hable (Ud.)
Hablen (Uds.) } Speak

comer
Coma (Ud.)
Coman (Uds.) } Eat

vivir
Viva (Ud.)
Vivan (Uds.) } Live

Negative Formal Commands

hablar
No hable (Ud.)
No hablen (Uds.) } Don't speak.

comer
No coma (Ud.)
No coman (Uds.) } Don't eat.

vivir
No viva (Ud.)
No vivan (Uds.) } Don't live.

Compre el libro.	Buy the book.
No compre el libro.	Don't buy the book.
Beba la leche.	Drink the milk.
No beba la leche.	Don't drink the milk.
Escríbala mañana.	Write it tomorrow.
No la escriba hoy.	Don't write it today.
Dígame la verdad.	Tell me the truth.
No me diga eso.	Don't tell me that.
Hágalo hoy.	Do it today.
No lo haga mañana.	Don't do it tomorrow.
Vaya con su hermana.	Go with your sister.
No vaya con Roberto.	Don't go with Robert.
Váyase.	Go away.
No se vaya.	Don't go away.
Póngalo en la mesa.	Put it on the table.
No lo ponga en la silla.	Don't put it on the chair.
Pónganlos aquí.	Put them here.
No los pongan allí.	Don't put them there.
Salgan temprano.	Leave early.
No salgan tarde.	Don't leave late.
Sea bueno.	Be good.
No sea malo.	Don't be bad.
Tenga paciencia.	Be patient.
No tenga miedo.	Don't be afraid.
Venga el lunes.	Come on Monday.
No venga el viernes.	Don't come on Friday.
Vengan todos.	All come.
No vengan.	Don't come.

13. Passive Voice

If a subject performs an action, the verb is active.

If the subject receives the action or is acted upon, the verb is passive.

The past participle of a verb is used with *ser* to form the passive construction and is called the passive voice.

The verb *ser* may be used in any tense. The past participle always agrees with the subject in number and gender.

> **La madre castiga al niño.** (active)
> **El niño es castigado.** (passive)

Passive Voice

Present

castigar

I am punished, you are punished, he is punished, etc.

soy castigado, -a	somos castigados, -as
eres castigado, -a	sois castigados, -as
es castigado, -a	son castigados, -as

When the past participle is used with *estar,* it is considered a predicate adjective and must agree in number and gender with what it modifies.

La casa fue destruida **por el viento.**	The house was destroyed by the wind. (passive)
Cuando la vi, la casa **estaba destruida.**	When I saw it, the house was destroyed. (predicate adj.)

The agent is expressed by *por* if the action is physical; if mental, *de* is preferred.

El niño fue castigado *por* **su** **padre.**	The boy was punished by his father.
Rosa es amada *de* **todos.**	Rose is loved by all.

Reflexive Substitute for the Passive

The reflexive form *se* is generally used, instead of the real passive construction, when the subject is an inanimate object and when no agent is expressed. If the agent is expressed, the passive is preferred.

The word *se* is not used as a reflexive; it replaces the verb *ser* and is so translated. The verb which follows *se* replaces the past participle of the passive. It is always the third person singular or plural, and may be used in any tense. The subject usually follows the verb.

Aquí se habla español.	Spanish is spoken here.
Se garantiza el trabajo.	The work is guaranteed.
¿Se venden sellos aquí?	Are stamps sold here?
Se publicaban libros.	Books were published.
Se venderá la casa.	The house will be sold.
Se vendió la casa.	The house was sold.
Se vendió.	It was sold.
La casa se ha vendido.	The house has been sold.
Las casas se han vendido.	The houses have been sold.
Las casas se habían vendido.	The houses had been sold.
El fuego se apagó.	The fire was put out. (went out)
El fuego fue apagado por el viento.	The fire was put out by the wind.

Many times the same meaning can be expressed by using the third person plural of the verb.

Hablan español en México.	They speak Spanish in Mexico.
Se habla español en México.	Spanish is spoken in Mexico.
Cultivan el algodón.	They cultivate cotton.
Se cultiva el algodón.	Cotton is cultivated.

Impersonal Use of *Se*

Se is used with the third person singular of a verb to express an indefinite it, they, one, or you.

Se dice,	It is said (they say, one says)
¿Cómo se dice?	How do you say?
Se cree,	It is believed
No se sabe,	It is not known
¿Por dónde se va?	How does one go? (How do you go?)

Reflexive Substitute with a Person as Subject

Although the passive voice is generally used when the subject is a person, the reflexive substitute may also be used. If so used, the person is made the object of the verb, which is always third person singular.

La piedra fue levantada.	The stone was raised.
Se levantó la piedra.	

La niña fue levantada. Se levantó a la niña. }	The girl was raised.
Se la levantó.	She was raised.
Se le levantó.	He was raised.
Los niños fueron levantados. Se levantó a los niños. }	The boys were raised.
Se les levantó.	They were raised.
Se las levantó.	They were raised. (f.)
Se registró la maleta.	The suitcase was searched.
Se registró al hombre.	The man was searched.
Se registraron las maletas.	The suitcases were searched..
Se registró a los hombres.	The men were searched.
Se considera bonita.	She considers herself pretty.
Se la considera bonita.	She is considered pretty.
Se consideran inteligentes.	They consider themselves intelligent.
Se les considera inteligentes.	They are considered intelligent.
A Juan se le admira.	John is admired.
A Rosa se la adora.	Rose is adored.
Se me envió a Panamá.	I was sent to Panama.
Se nos envió a Italia.	We were sent to Italy.
Se les daba dinero.	They were given money.
Se le dio el nombre de su tío.	He was given the name of his uncle.

14. Impersonal Verbs

Impersonal verbs are those which are used only in the third person singular, with no definite subject.

Haber used impersonally expresses existence.

Haber

Indicative

Simple Tenses

Present	1. **hay**	there is, there are
Imperfect	2. **había**	there was, there were
Preterite	3. **hubo**	there was, there were
Future	4. **habrá**	there will be
Conditional	5. **habría**	there would be

Perfect Tenses

Pres. Perfect	1. **ha habido**	there has been
Past Perfect	2. **había habido**	there had been
Pret. Perfect	3. **hubo habido**	there had been
Fut. Perfect	4. **habrá habido**	there will have been
Cond. Perfect	5. **habría habido**	there would have been

Subjunctive

Present	1. **haya**	there may be
Past	2. **hubiera** **hubiese**	there might or should be
Pres. Perfect	3. **haya habido**	there may have been
Past Perfect	4. **hubiera** **hubiese** } **habido**	there might or should have been

Hay **flores en la mesa.**	There are flowers on the table.
Había **muchas flores en el jardín.**	There were many flowers in the garden.
Ayer *hubo* **una tempestad.**	Yesterday there was a storm.
Habrá **frutas en el verano.**	There will be fruit in the summer.
Ha habido **muchos temblores en Chile.**	They have been many earthquakes in Chile.

Weather Verbs

Weather verbs are impersonal, being used only in the third person singular of the various tenses, with no subject expressed.

Llover to rain

Indicative
Simple Tenses

Present	1. **llueve**	it rains, it is raining
Imperfect	2. **llovía**	it used to rain, it was raining
Preterite	3. **llovió**	it rained
Future	4. **lloverá**	it will rain
Conditional	5. **llovería**	it would rain

Perfect Tenses

Pres. Perfect	1. **ha llovido**	it has rained
Past Perfect	2. **había llovido**	it had rained
Pret. Perfect	3. **hubo llovido**	it had rained
Fut. Perfect	4. **habrá llovido**	it will have rained
Cond. Perfect	5. **habría llovido**	it would have rained

Subjunctive

Present	1. **llueva**	it may rain
Past	2. **lloviera** **lloviese**	it might or should rain
Pres. Perfect	3. **haya llovido**	it may have rained
Past Perfect	4. **hubiera** **hubiese** llovido	it might or should have rained

amanecer	to dawn
anochecer	to grow dark
granizar	to hail
helar (ie)	to freeze
llover (ue)	to rain
lloviznar	to drizzle
nevar (ie)	to snow
relampaguear	to lighten
tronar (ue)	to thunder

Hacer and *haber* are used impersonally in many weather idioms. They are then translated to be.

hacer frío to be cold	**hacer calor** to be warm

Hace frío.	It is cold.
Hacía calor.	It was warm.
Hará frío.	It will be cold.

Haber is used in weather idioms when the expression refers to something visible.

Hay luna.	The moon is shining
Hay polvo.	It is dusty.

15. Idiomatic Verbs

The verbs *gustar, faltar, quedar,* and *doler* take an indirect object. The subject in English becomes the object in Spanish or vice versa.

If something pleases you in Spanish, you like it in English. The object *it* of the verb in English is understood in Spanish; therefore, it is never expressed. The object in the English sentence (the subject of the Spanish sentence) determines the number of the verb.

gustar   to please, to give pleasure to

Me **gusta** *el libro.*	I like the book. (The book gives pleasure to me.)
Me **gustan** *los libros.*	I like the books. (The books give pleasure to me.)

Present

The book pleases me; I like the book; you like the book, etc.

Me gusta el libro.	**Nos gusta el libro.**
Te gusta el libro.	**Os gusta el libro.**
Le gusta el libro.	**Les gusta el libro.**

The meaning of *le* and *les* may be made clear by the addition of the forms *a Ud., a él, a ella; a Uds., a ellos, a ellas.*

Me gusta la casa.	I like the house.
Me gusta.	I like it.
No me gusta.	I do not like it.
¿Le gusta a Ud.?	Do you like it?
Nos gustan las flores.	We like flowers.
Les gustó la comida.	They liked the dinner.
Le gustaba a ella viajar.	She liked to travel.

faltar   to be lacking, to be in need of

Me falta el dinero para el viaje.	I lack the money for the trip.
Les faltaban los libros necesarios.	They lacked the necessary books.
Les faltan muchas cosas.	They need many things.

quedar to have left over

Me queda un peso.	I have a dollar left.
Le quedan dos periódicos.	He has two newspapers left.
¿Cuánto le queda a Ud.?	How much do you have left?
Después de pagar la cuenta, le quedarán a Ud. tres pesos.	After paying the bill, you will have three dollars left.

doler to ache, to pain

My head aches, your head aches, etc.

Me duele la cabeza.	**Nos duele la cabeza.**
Te duele la cabeza.	**Os duele la cabeza.**
Le duele la cabeza.	**Les duele la cabeza.**
Me duelen los ojos.	My eyes hurt.
Le duelen los pies.	His feet ache.

caber to be contained in

If an object is contained in something in Spanish, the thing in which it is contained holds it in English.

The object of the preposition in Spanish becomes the subject in English, or vice versa.

Caben diez personas en el as-censor.	There is room for ten persons, or The elevator holds ten persons.
En esta bolsa cabe mucho.	This purse holds a great deal.

hacer expressing a period of time

Hacer is commonly used in expressions of time in the third person singular of the present, imperfect, and future. The tense is determined by the point of time from which the period of time is reckoned.

When a past tense is followed by a time phrase in the present, it is translated as ago.

La *vi* **hace dos meses.**	I saw her two months ago.
Estuve **en México hace un año.**	I was in Mexico a year ago.
Lo *hice* **hace mucho tiempo.**	I did it a long time ago.

The same thought is expressed by placing the time phrase first followed by *que*, which may be translated since.

Hace un año que la vi.	It is a year since I saw her. / I saw her a year ago.
Hace un año que estuve en México.	It is a year since I was in Mexico. / I was in Mexico a year ago.

If the time phrase is in the present followed by the present, the action is still going on.

Hace un año que *vivo* **aquí.**	I have been living here a year.
Hace dos años que Elena *estudia* **el español.**	Helen has been studying Spanish for two years.
Hace mucho tiempo que no la *veo.* **(he visto)***	I have not seen her for a long time.
¿Cuánto tiempo hace que Ud. *está* **aquí?**	How long have you been here?

*The present perfect may be used in a negative expression.

If the time phrase is in the imperfect followed by the imperfect, the action was going on in the past.

Hacía un año que yo estudiaba el español.	I had been studying Spanish a year.
Hacía un mes que vivíamos allí.	We had been living there for a month.

Imperfect + past perfect

Hacía entonces dos años que había partido.	It was then two years since he had left.
Hacía un año que yo no la había visto.	I had not seen her for a year.

16. Verbs Followed by a Preposition

The following verbs require a preposition when used before an infinitive. The preposition is not always translated.

a

acostumbrarse a   to become used to
aprender a   to learn to
atreverse a   to dare to
ayudar a   to help
comenzar a   to begin to
convidar a   to invite to
decidirse a   to decide to
dedicarse a   to devote oneself to
empezar a   to begin to
enseñar a   to teach to
invitar a   to invite to
ir a   to go to
negarse a   to refuse to
persuadir a   to persuade to
principiar a   to begin to
rehusar a   to refuse to
resignarse a   to resign oneself to
resistirse a   to resist
resolverse a   to resolve to
venir a   to come to
volver a   to return to; to do—
   again

con

contar con   to count on
contentarse con   to content oneself with
soñar con   to dream of

de

acabar de   to have just
acordarse de   to remember
alegrarse de   to be glad to
aprovecharse de   to profit by
arrepentirse de   to repent
cansarse de   to tire of
cesar de   to cease
dejar de   to cease
encargarse de   to take charge of
gozar de   to take pleasure in
jactarse de   to boast of
olvidarse de   to forget to
tratar de   to try to

en

consentir en   to consent to
consistir en   to consist
divertirse en   to amuse oneself
empeñarse en   to insist on
esforzarse en   to endeavor to
insistir en   to insist on
ocuparse en   to busy oneself
pensar en   to think of
persistir en   to persist in
tardar en   to delay in

Aprendo a hablar español.
No me atrevo a hacerlo.

I am learning to speak Spanish.
I do not dare do it.

Me alegro de saberlo.
Juan trata de hacerlo.

I am glad to know it.
John is trying to do it.

María insiste en ir.	Mary insists on going.
No tardó en hacerlo.	He did not delay in doing it.
Contaré con verle.	I shall count on seeing you.
Sueña con volar.	He dreams of flying.

Part Two:
Essentials of Grammar

17. The Article

	Singular	Plural	
Definite Article, the	*el*	*los*	(*m.*)
	la	*las*	(*f.*)
Indefinite Article, a, an, some	*un*	*unos*	(*m.*)
	una	*unas*	(*f.*)

The articles agree in number and gender with the noun.

Singular	Plural
el libro the book	**los libros** the books
la pluma the pen	**las plumas** the pens
un libro a book	**unos libros** some books
una pluma a pen	**unas plumas** some pens

The masculine article in the singular is used before feminine words beginning with stressed *a* or *ha*.

el agua the water	**las aguas** the waters
el alma the soul	**las almas** the souls
el hada the fairy	**las hadas** the fairies

Contractions:

a + *el* = *al*	**Hablo** *al* **niño.**	I speak to the child.
de + *el* = *del*	**Hablo** *del* **niño.**	I speak of the child.

Uses

The definite article is used with:

1. Titles. The definite article is used before *señor, señora, señorita* and other titles, except *don* and *doña,* when speaking of a person, but not when speaking to the person.

El **señor Moreno es mi maestro.**	Mr. Moreno is my teacher.
Buenos días, señor Moreno.	Good morning, Mr. Moreno.
La **señorita García enseña el español.**	Miss García teaches Spanish.
El **capitán López es valiente.**	Captain López is valiant.
Don Juan es famoso.	Don Juan is famous.
El **señor don José García es rico.**	Mr. Joseph García is rich.

2. Nouns used in a general sense.

El oro **es precioso.**	Gold is precious.
El azúcar **es dulce.**	Sugar is sweet.
Los perros **son fieles.**	Dogs are faithful.

3. Languages. The article is generally used with the names of languages except when placed directly after the verb *hablar* or the prepositions *en* or *de*.

Pablo estudia *el* **inglés.**	Paul is studying English.
Pablo habla español.	Paul speaks Spanish.
Habla bien *el* **español.**	He speaks Spanish well.
Escribe la lección de inglés.	He writes the English lesson.
Escribe la lección en inglés.	He writes the lesson in English.

4. Parts of the body or clothing.

Carmen tiene *los* **ojos azules.**	Carmen has blue eyes.
Pedro tiene *el* **pelo negro.**	Peter has black hair.
María se puso *el* **sombrero.**	Mary put on her hat.

5. Units of measure.

Costó dos pesos *el* **metro.**	It cost two dollars a meter.
Se vende a diez centavos *la* **libra.**	It is sold at ten cents a pound.

Omission of the Article

The indefinite article is omitted before an unmodified predicate noun denoting nationality, occupation, or rank.

Es americano.	**Es** *un buen* **americano.**
He is an American.	He is a good American.
Es médico.	**Es** *un médico* **famoso.**
He is a doctor.	He is a famous doctor.
Es general.	**Es** *un gran* **general.**
He is a general.	He is a great general.

The definite article is omitted:
1. Before a noun in apposition.

La Habana, capital de Cuba, es una ciudad hermosa.	Havana, the capital of Cuba, is a beautiful city.

Note: The article is used if the noun is followed by an adjective in the superlative degree.

La Habana, la ciudad más hermosa de Cuba, es la capital.	Havana, the most beautiful city of Cuba, is the capital.

2. Before a numeral used with the name of a ruler.

Felipe Cuarto	Phillip the Fourth
Alfonso Trece	Alfonso the Thirteenth

Neuter Article, *Lo*

1. *Lo* is used before a masculine singular adjective, a past participle or a possessive, to express their value in an abstract sense (to form abstract nouns).

lo bueno the good	**lo ocurrido** what happened
lo útil what is useful	**lo mío** what is mine
lo hecho what is done	**lo suyo** what is yours, his, etc.

Llevaré sólo lo necesario.	I shall take only what is necessary.
Lo mío es suyo.	What is mine is yours.

2. *lo* + adjective or adverb + *que,* how

The adjective agrees in gender and number with the noun to which it refers.

lo bueno que how good	**lo bien que** how well

Ud. no sabe lo inteligentes que son.	You do not know how intelligent they are.
El no sabe lo bien que lo ha hecho Juan.	He does not know how well John has done it.

18. Nouns

Gender and Number

Gender

All nouns in Spanish are either masculine or feminine. The gender of those denoting person or animals is determined by the sex.

el hombre   the man   **la mujer**   the woman

Nouns ending in -*o* are usually masculine and those ending in -*a, -dad, -ión, -umbre*, are usually feminine.

el libro   the book   **la pluma**   the pen   **la verdad**   the truth
la nación   the nation   **la costumbre**   the custom

Many nouns form the feminine by changing the final -*o* of the masculine to *a*, others by adding *a* to the masculine form.

el maestro, la maestra
el profesor, la profesora   } the teacher

Number

1. The plural of nouns is formed by adding -*s* to words ending in an unaccented vowel and -*es* to those ending in a consonant or an accented vowel.

la casa   house   **las casas**   houses
el papel   paper   **los papeles**   papers
el rubí   ruby   **los rubíes**   rubies
el bambú   bamboo   **los bambúes**   bamboos

Exceptions:

el papá, los papás; la mamá, las mamás; el sofá, los sofás

2. Words ending in *z* change *z* to *c* when adding -*es*.

el lápiz   pencil   **los lápices**   pencils
la cruz   cross   **las cruces**   crosses

3. Words of more than one syllable ending in -*s* remain unchanged, unless the last syllable is stressed.

el mes month	**los meses** months
el lunes Monday	**los lunes** Mondays
el paraguas umbrella	**los paraguas** umbrellas
el inglés Englishman	**los ingleses** English
el francés Frenchman	**los franceses** French

4. Family names remain unchanged.

Los García   The Garcías

5. Nouns of relationship and rank, when used in the masculine plural, have two meanings.

los padres	fathers, parents
los hermanos	brothers, the brother and sister
los señores	men, Mr. and Mrs.
los reyes	kings, the king and queen

6. Abstract nouns, made by placing *lo* before an adjective, are neuter in gender and have no plural form.

lo bueno   the good   **lo malo**   the bad

19. Adjectives and Adverbs

Adjectives

Agreement

An adjective agrees in number and in gender with the noun or pronoun it modifies, whether as a direct modifier or as a predicate adjective. An adjective modifying nouns of different gender is in the masculine plural.

el libro rojo	the red book
la mesa roja	the red table
los libros rojos	the red books
las mesas rojas	the red tables
El libro es rojo.	The book is red.
La mesa es roja.	The table is red.
Los libros son rojos.	The books are red.
Las mesas son rojas.	The tables are red.
El libro y la mesa son rojos.	The book and the table are red.

Number

The plural of adjectives is formed by adding -s to words ending in a vowel, and -es to those ending in a consonant.

rojo, rojos, azul, azules

Gender

Adjectives ending in -o are masculine. They change -o to -a to form the feminine.

el libro rojo	the red book	los libros rojos	the red books
la pluma roja	the red pen	las plumas rojas	the red pens

Adjectives of nationality and those ending in -an, -on, and -or (except the comparatives mejor, peor, mayor, and menor) add -a to form the feminine. All others have the same form for both genders.

español, española	Spanish
holgazán, holgazana	lazy
preguntón, preguntona	inquisitive
hablador, habladora	talkative

Position

A descriptive adjective usually follows the noun. Some adjectives have a different meaning, according to their position with reference to the noun.

el hombre pobre	the poor man (without money)
el pobre hombre	the poor man (unfortunate)

Shortened Forms

The following adjectives drop the final -*o* if placed before a masculine noun in the singular.

> **bueno,** good; **malo,** bad; **alguno,** some; **ninguno,** no, any;
> **uno,** one; **primero,** first; **tercero,** third
> **un hombre bueno, un buen hombre,** a good man

grande

When meaning great, *grande* precedes the noun and drops -*de* before a singular noun of either gender.

un gran general, a great general	**una gran actriz,** a great actress
unos grandes generales	**unas grandes actrices**

santo

Santo drops -*to* before all masculine names except those beginning with *Do-* or *To-*.

San José Saint Joseph	**Santo Domingo** Saint Dominic
San Francisco Saint Francis	**Santo Tomás** Saint Thomas

-ísimo

The suffix -*ísimo* (-*a*, -*os*, -*as*), very, may be used with an adjective instead of the word *muy* (very). It is added to the adjective, omitting the final vowel if there is one. This form is called the absolute superlative, although there is no idea of comparison.

muy grande, grandísimo,	**muy fácil, facilísimo,**
very large	very easy

mismo (-a, -os, -as) same, self (emphatic)

When meaning the same, the appropriate form of *mismo* precedes a noun. When used for emphasis, it follows a noun or pronoun.

No viven en la *misma* **casa.**	They do not live in the same house.
El *mismo* **lo hizo.**	He himself did it. He did it himself.

Definite article + adjective = noun

When any form of the definite article is placed before an adjective, the latter becomes a noun.

el pobre the poor man	**los pobres** the poor (people)
el joven the youth	**los jóvenes** the young people

lo + adjective = abstract noun

If the neuter article *lo* is placed before a masculine adjective in the singular, the latter becomes an abstract noun.

lo bueno the good (whatever is good)   **lo malo** the bad

lo + adj. + *que*   how
In such constructions the adjective agrees in number and gender with the noun or pronoun to which it refers.

lo bonito que   how pretty

lo tonto que   how silly

El no sabe lo interesante que es.   He does not know how interesting it is.

Ud. no sabe lo bonitas que son.   You do not know how pretty they are.

Descriptive Adjectives

grande large	**alto** high; tall
pequeño small	**bajo** low; short
largo long	**lindo, bonito** pretty
corto short	**hermoso** beautiful
bueno good	**feo** ugly
malo bad	**ancho** wide
rico rich	**angosto, estrecho** narrow
pobre poor	**pesado** heavy
fuerte strong	**ligero** light
débil weak	**negro** black
fácil easy	**blanco** white
difícil difficult	**rojo, colorado** red
gordo fat	**azul** blue
delgado thin, slender	**verde** green
duro hard	**amarillo** yellow
blando soft	**morado** purple
dulce sweet	**café** brown
agrio sour	**rosa** pink
amargo bitter	**anaranjado** orange color

Comparison of Adjectives

To form the comparative, place *más* (more) or *menos* (less) before the adjective. To form the superlative, place the definite article before the comparative.

Positive	Comparative	Superlative
dulce sweet	*más* **dulce** sweeter	*el más* **dulce** ⎫ *la más* **dulce** ⎭ the sweetest
altos tall	*más* **altos** taller	*los más* **altos** the tallest

In the superlative the most usual form is to place the article before the noun, when it is expressed.

Rosa es *la más alta.*   Rose is the tallest.

Rosa es *la niña más alta.*   Rose is the tallest girl.

A possessive may be used instead of the article.

Rosa es *mi* hermana más alta.   Rose is my tallest sister.

De is used to express in after a superlative.

**Rosa es la niña más bonita *de*   Rose is the prettiest girl in the
la clase.**   class.

Irregular Comparison

Bueno, malo, grande, and *pequeño* have irregular comparisons. The irregular comparisons of *grande* and *pequeño* are used when they refer to importance or age rather than size.

Positive		Comparative		Superlative	
bueno, -a **buenos, -as** } good		**mejor** **mejores** } better		**el (la) mejor** **los (las) mejores** } the best	
malo, -a **malos, -as** } bad		**peor** **peores** } worse		**el (la) peor** **los (las) peores** } the worst	
grande great, large		**mayor** greater, older		**el mayor** **la mayor** } the greatest or the oldest	
pequeño, -a small		**menor** less, younger		**el menor** **la menor** } the least, the youngest	

**Juan es más grande que su   John is larger than his older
hermano mayor.**   brother.

Comparatives

1. Inequality

que   than
más ___ que   more than   **menos ___ que**   less than

**El elefante es *más* fuerte   The elephant is stronger than
que el caballo.**   the horse.
**El gato es *menos* inteligente   The cat is less intelligent than
que el perro.**   the dog.

De is used before a number after an affirmative statement. After a negative statement either *de* or *que* may be used but preferably *que*.

Trabajó más *de* dos días.   He worked more than two days.
No **trabajó más *que* dos días.** He did not work more than two
                                      days.

2. Equality

tan ___ **como**	as ___ as	**Juan es** *tan* **alto** *como* **usted.**	John is as tall as you.
tanto(-a) ___ **como**	as much ___ as	**Tiene** *tanto* **dinero** *como* **yo.**	He has as much money as I.
tantos(-as) ___ **como**	as many ___ as	**Tengo** *tantas* **amigas** *como* **ella.**	I have as many friends as she.

Than followed by a clause: When than is followed by a clause, it is expressed by *del que, de la que, de los que,* and *de las que,* if the comparison is based upon a noun of the preceding clause. If it is based upon the whole idea of the preceding clause, than is expressed by *de lo que.*

María tiene más *libros* *de los que* **ha traído.**	Mary has more books than she has brought.
Juan es más fuerte de lo que **creían.**	John is stronger than they thought.

Comparisons with either adjectives or adverbs

más que nunca	more than ever	**Tiene más dinero que nunca.**
mejor que nunca	better than ever	**Canta mejor que nunca.**
más que nadie	more than anyone	**Gana más dinero que nadie.**
mejor que nadie	better than anyone	**Canta mejor que nadie.**

Ratio

cuanto más ___ **(tanto) más**	the more ___ the more
cuanto más ___ **(tanto) menos**	the more ___ the less
cuanto menos ___ **(tanto) más**	the less ___ the more
cuanto menos ___ **(tanto) menos**	the less ___ the less

Cuanto más dinero tiene, (tanto) más quiere.	The more money he has, the more he wants.
Cuanto más gana, menos tiene.	The more he earns, the less he has.

Adverbs

Position

The position of adverbs is usually determined by the meaning. Many adverbs may either precede or follow the verb.

Ayer la vi.	**La vi ayer.**	I saw her yesterday.

-mente -ly

Many adverbs are formed by adding the suffix *-mente* (equivalent to -ly in English) to the feminine form of the adjective, if there is one.

correcto, -a **correct***amente* correctly	**fácil** **fácil***mente* *easily*

-ísimo   very

The suffix *-ísimo*, when joined to an adverb, is equivalent to the word *muy,* very, placed before it. When added, the final vowel of the adverb is omitted (if there is one).

temprano tempran*ísimo*
very early

pronto pront*ísimo*
very soon

lo + adv. + *que*   expresses how

lo bien que   how well

lo mucho   how much

Usted no sabe lo bien que canta.

You do not know how well she sings.

Usted no sabe lo mucho que lo aprecio.

You do not know how much I appreciate it.

lo más + adv. + an expression of possibility   as ___ as ___

Lo más can be placed before an adverb and followed by some word or expression of possibility.

lo más pronto posible
lo más temprano posible

as soon as possible
as early as possible

Lo haré lo más pronto posible.
Venga lo más pronto posible.

I shall do it as soon as possible.
Come as soon as possible.

Comparison of Adverbs

The regular comparison is formed like that of adjectives, by placing *más* or *menos* before the adverb.

The superlative is generally the same as the comparative.

Juan anda aprisa. (positive)
Pedro anda más aprisa. (comparative)
Pablo es el que anda más aprisa. (superlative)

John walks fast.
Peter walks faster.
Paul is the one who walks the fastest, (Paul walks the fastest.)

Irregular Comparisons

Only four adverbs, *bien, mal, mucho,* and *poco* have irregular comparisons.

bien   well; **mejor**   better, best
mucho   much; **más**   more, most

mal   badly; **peor**   worse, worst
poco   little; **menos**   less, least

Juan habla bien.
Pablo habla mejor.
Tomás es el que habla mejor.

John speaks well.
Paul speaks better.
Thomas speaks the best.

20. Demonstrative Adjectives and Pronouns

Demonstrative Adjectives

Singular		Plural	
este (*m.*) esta (*f.*) } this		estos estas } these	
ese (*m.*) esa (*f.*) } that		esos esas } those	
aquel (*m.*) aquella (*f.*) } that		aquellos aquellas } those	

Demonstrative adjectives precede and agree in number and gender with the noun they modify.

Ese and not *aquel* is used when referring to what is near the person addressed; *aquel* is used when referring to what is remote from both the speaker and the one addressed.

este libro	this book
ese libro que Ud. tiene	that book you have
aquel árbol en el jardín	that tree in the garden
esta semana; esos años	this week; those years
aquel siglo	that century

Demonstrative Pronouns

Singular	Plural
éste ⎫ this, this one ésta ⎭	éstos ⎫ these éstas ⎭
ése ⎫ that, that one ésa ⎭	ésos ⎫ those ésas ⎭
aquél ⎫ that, that one aquélla ⎭	aquéllos ⎫ those aquéllas ⎭
esto this eso, aquello that } neuter forms	

The neuter forms do not have the accent because there are no corresponding adjective forms. The neuter forms refer to an idea, a whole statement, or anything not specifically mentioned by name.

The demonstrative pronouns have a written accent over the *e* of the stressed syllable to distinguish them from the adjectives which have the same form. They agree in number and gender with the noun for which they stand.

Este libro es por Galdós, y ése es por Valera.	This book is by Galdos, and that one is by Valera.
Esta construcción es un templo; aquélla es una fortaleza.	This structure is a temple; that one is a fortress.
¿Qué es esto?	What is this?
¿Quién dijo eso?	Who said that?
Aquello no tenía importancia.	That had no importance.

The demonstrative pronoun before *que* or *de* is usually replaced by the definite article.

Este libro es bueno pero (ése) el que Ud. tiene es mejor.	This book is good but that one you have is better.
(Aquéllos) los que vienen son sus amigos.	Those who are coming are his friends.
El sombrero de María y el de su amiga son bonitos.	Mary's hat and that of her friend are pretty.

The former, the latter. The different forms *éste, ésta, éstos, -as* may also mean the latter, and *aquél, aquélla, aquéllos, -as,* the former.

María y Rosa son primas; *ésta* es rubia, *aquélla* es morena.	Mary and Rose are cousins; the latter is blond, the former is brunette.
Alicia y José son españoles; *éste* es de Madrid, *aquélla* de Sevilla.	Alice and Joseph are Spanish; the former is from Seville, the latter from Madrid.
Eduardo es más grande que Carlos, pero *éste* es el mayor.	Edward is larger than Charles, but the latter is the older.

21. Possessive Adjectives and Pronouns

Possessive Adjectives

Possessive adjectives are placed before the noun and agree in number and in gender with the thing possessed, not the possessor.

mi, mis my	**nuestro, nuestros** **nuestra, nuestras** } our	
tu, tus your	**vuestro, vuestros** **vuestra, vuestras** } your	
su, sus your, his, her	**su, sus** your, their	

mi libro	my book
mi mesa	my table
mis hermanos	my brothers
mis hermanas	my sisters
nuestra mesa	our table
nuestros libros	our books
su libro	your (his, her) book
sus mesas	your (their) tables
el libro de Ud.	your book
el libro de él	his book
el libro de ella	her book
los libros de ella	her books
el libro de ellos	their (*m.*) book
los libros de ellos	their (*m.*) books
las mesas de ellos	their (*m.*) tables

Because *su* and *sus* can have many different meanings, the definite article may be used instead of *su* with the following forms: *de Ud., de él, de ella; de Uds., de ellos, de ellas.*

los libros de ellos   their books

The definite article is used instead of the possessive adjective when speaking of parts of the body or articles of clothing when the thing belongs to or is a part of the subject and when the possession is obvious.

Ella se pone *el* **sombrero.**	She puts on her hat.
Juan levanta *la* **mano.**	John raises his hand.
El mete *la* **mano en el bolsillo.**	He puts his hand in his pocket.

Terminal Forms

The following forms of the possessive adjectives are placed after the noun, which must be preceded by the definite article, except in direct address.

mío, -a	**míos, -as**	**nuestro, -a**	**nuestros, -as**
tuyo, a	**tuyos, -as**	**vuestro, -a**	**vuestros, -as**
suyo, -a	**suyos, -as**	**suyo, -a**	**suyos, -as**

mi libro, el libro *mío*   my book
su casa, la casa *suya*   your house
¿Qué haces, hijo *mío*?   What are you doing, my son?

The indefinite article, when used with the terminal forms, corresponds to the English meaning of mine, of yours, etc.

un **amigo** *mío*   a friend of mine
una **amiga** *nuestra*   a friend of ours

Possessive Pronouns

The possessive pronouns are always preceded by the definite article, except after the verb *ser,* when it may be omitted. These pronouns agree in number and gender with the thing possessed.

el mío, los míos **la mía, las mías** } mine		**el nuestro, los nuestros** **la nuestra, las nuestras** } ours	
el tuyo, los tuyos **la tuya, las tuyas** } yours		**el vuestro, los vuestros** **la vuestra, las vuestras** } yours	
el suyo, los suyos **la suya, las suyas** } yours, his, hers		**el suyo, los suyos** **la suya, las suyas** } yours, theirs	

To avoid ambiguity, the third person forms, *el suyo, la suya,* etc., are usually replaced by the following phrases.

el de Ud., el de él, el de ella; el de Uds., el de ellos, el de ellas

El suyo es rojo. His is red.

El de ella **es rojo.** Hers is red.

El vestido *de ella* **es rojo;**
 el mío es azul.

Her dress is red;
 mine is blue.

Mi casa es pequeña;
 la suya es grande.

My house is small; (yours, <br> his, hers, theirs) is large.

Nuestra casa es blanca;
 la de él **es verde.**

Our house is white;
 his is green.

Lo + possessive: When *lo* is placed before the masculine singular form of any of the possessives, it has the meaning whatever is mine, whatever is yours, etc.

Lo mío **es suyo y** *lo suyo* **es mío.**   Whatever is mine is his, and <br> whatever is his, is mine.

22. Object Pronouns

Direct Object Pronouns

The direct object pronoun receives the action of the verb.

Singular		Plural	
me	me	**nos**	us
te	you	**os**	you
le, lo (*m.*)	you, him	**les, los**	you, them
la (*f.*)	you, her, it	**las**	you, them
lo (*m.*)	it	**los**	them
lo (*n.*)	it	

For clearness or emphasis with the third persons, the following explanations may be added.

To *le, lo, la:* **a Ud., a él, a ella**
To *les, los, las:* **a Uds., a ellos, a ellas**
    El *le* **ve** *a Ud.*   He sees you.   *Le* **ve** *a él.*   He sees him.

Indirect Object Pronouns

The indirect object pronoun denotes the person to, for, or from whom anything is given, told, sent, etc.

me	to me	**nos**	to us
te	to you	**os**	to you
le	to you, him, her, it	**les**	to you, them

For clearness or emphasis with the third persons, the following explanations may be added.

To *le:* **a Ud., a él, a ella**
To *les:* **a Uds., a ellos, a ellas**

No *le* **habló** *a ella.*   He didn't speak to her.
Les **mandó el libro** *a ellas.*   He sent them (*f.*) the book.

Reflexive Pronouns

A reflexive pronoun must always accompany a verb which is reflexive. A reflexive verb is one whose subject and object are the same; that is, the subject acts upon itself. A reflexive verb is indicated by the pronoun *se* attached to the infinitive.

me	myself	**nos**	ourselves
te	yourself	**os**	yourselves
se	yourself, herself, himself	**se**	yourselves, themselves

Me **siento.**	I sit down.
Te **vistes.**	You dress yourself.
Se **levantó.**	He got (himself) up.
Nos **acostamos.**	We went to bed.
Se **fueron.**	They went away.

Position of the Object Pronouns

An object pronoun (direct, indirect, or reflexive) generally precedes the conjugated verb.

Exceptions: The object pronoun follows and is attached to the verb if the latter is a direct affirmative command, or suggestion, an infinitive, or a gerund. It may precede an auxiliary verb used with an infinitive, or a gerund.

Juan *lo* **vio.**	John saw it.
No *lo* **vio.**	He did not see it.
Juan *le* **dio el libro.**	John gave him the book.
Juan *se* **levanta temprano.**	John rises early.
No *se* **levanta tarde.**	He does not rise late.
Dé*me* **Ud. el libro.**	Give me the book.
No *me* **dé el lápiz.**	Do not give me the pencil.
Leámos*lo.*	Let us read it.
No *lo* **escribamos.**	Let us not write it.
Me alegro de saber*lo.*	I am glad to know it.
Quiero hablar*le.* }	I wish to speak to him.
Le **quiero hablar.** }	
Estoy escribiéndo*la.* }	I am writing it.
La **estoy escribiendo.** }	

Note: When one or two object pronouns follow and are attached to the verb form, an accent mark must be added to retain the original stress of the verb.

Two Object Pronouns

When there are two object pronouns, the indirect precedes the direct. A reflexive precedes another pronoun. If both pronouns begin with the letter *l,* the first one is changed to *se* (*se lo* for *le lo, les lo,* etc.). Both pronouns precede the conjugated verb.

Exceptions: Both pronouns follow and are attached to the verb if the latter is an affirmative command, or suggestion, an infinitive, or a gerund. They may precede an auxiliary verb used with an infinitive, or a gerund. Their relative position always remains the same.

	He gave		He gave
Me lo dio.	it to me.	**Nos lo dio.**	it to us.
Te lo dio.	it to you.	**Os lo dio.**	it to you.
Se lo dio.	it to you, to him, to her.	**Se lo dio.**	it to you, to them.

For clearness or emphasis, the following prepositional forms may be used with either the direct or indirect object pronouns: *a mí, a ti, a Ud., a él, a ella; a nosotros, -as, a vosotros, -as, a ustedes, a ellos, a ellas.*

Juan se lo dio *a ella.*	John gave it to her.
No se lo dio *a él.*	He did not give it to him.
Déselo *a él.*	Give it to him.
Está dándoselo *a ella.*	He is giving it to her.
Quiero dárselas *a Ud.*	I want to give them to you.
Me las prometió *a mí.*	He promised them to me.
A mí **me las dio.**	He gave them to me.

When a verb has two pronoun objects, and the direct object is a pronoun of the first or second person, the indirect object is expressed with the prepositional form.

Me presentó *a ella.*	She introduced me to her.
¿**No te presentó** *a él?*	Did she not introduce you to him?
Me dirigí *a él.*	I addressed myself to him.
Me la envió.	He sent her to me.
Nos envió *a Ud.*	He sent us to you.

Note: When two pronoun objects, the first of which is *se (selo, sela,* etc.), are joined to an affirmative suggestion, the final letter of the verb is dropped.

Cantemos + se + la = Cantém*osela.*   Let us sing it to her.

Pronouns as Objects of a Preposition

mí	me	**nosotros, -as**	us
ti	you	**vosotros, -as**	you
Ud.	you	**Uds.**	you
él	him, it	**ellos**	them
ella	her, it	**ellas**	
ello	it (neuter)		
sí	yourself, himself, herself	**sí**	yourselves, themselves

Hablábamos *de él.*	We were speaking of him.
Las flores son *para ella.*	The flowers are for her.
Su padre insistió *en ello.*	His father insisted on it.

Con, with, combines with *mí, ti,* and *sí,* forming the words *conmigo,* with me; *contigo,* with you; *consigo,* with yourself, himself, herself, yourselves, themselves.

María va conmigo.	Mary is going with me.
Iré contigo.	I shall go with you.
¿Tiene Ud. el libro consigo?	Have you the book with you?
No tenían dinero consigo.	They had no money with them.

mismo, -a, -os, -as   self, selves

For clearness or emphasis, the appropriate forms of *mismo* may be added to the prepositional pronouns.

Habla demasiado de *sí misma.*	She talks too much of herself.
Se engañaron a *sí mismos.*	They deceived themselves.
Me aborrezco a *mí mismo.*	I hate myself.

Prepositions Commonly Used With Pronouns:

a	to	**al lado de**	beside
con	with	**alrededor de**	around
contra	against	**cerca de**	near
de	of, from	**lejos de**	far from
en	in, on	**delante de**	in front of
entre	between, among	**enfrente de**	in front of
*para	for	**detrás de**	behind
por	for	**encima de**	above
sobre	on, over	**debajo de**	below, under

**Para,* when it is used with *mí, ti, sí,* after some verbs, is translated as oneself.

Dijo para sí:	He said to himself,
Juró para sí que . . .	He swore to himself that . . .
Dije para mí	I said to myself,

23. Relative Pronouns

A relative pronoun is one that joins a dependent clause to the main clause and refers to something previously mentioned in the sentence (the antecedent).

The relative pronoun may serve as the subject or object of a verb, or as the object of a preposition. *Que* and *quien* are the relatives most commonly used.

Pronouns as Relatives

1. *Que,* who, whom, that, or which may refer to persons or things, except after a preposition, when it refers to things only.

La niña *que* canta es mi prima.	The girl who is singing is my cousin.
La niña *que* Ud. vio es su prima.	The girl whom you saw is his cousin.
El libro *que* tengo es la gramá-tica.	The book that I have is the grammar.
La casa en *que* vivo es grande.	The house in which I live is large.

El que (la que, los que, las que) and *el cual (la cual, los cuales, las cuales)* may replace *que* or *quien,* referring to persons.or things. These pronouns are used for clearness when there are two possible antecedents. They are also used with prepositions, especially those of more than one syllable.

La prima de Juan, *la cual (la que)* vivía en Cuba, está aquí.	John's cousin, who used to live in Cuba, is here.
He visitado la ciudad cerca de *la cual* vive.	I have visited the city near which he lives.

2. *Quien, -es* (persons only), who, is used only in a supplementary or non-essential clause.

Hablé con Rosa, *quien* es muy inteligente.	I talked with Rose, who is very intelligent.

Quien, -es when used with a preposition, means whom.

La niña *a quien* **hablé es su prima.**	The girl to whom I spoke is his cousin.
La niña *de quien* **habló es su prima.**	The girl of whom he spoke is his cousin.

3. *Lo que* and *lo cual*, which, refers to the whole statement.

Lo hizo, *lo que* **me sorprendió.**	He did it, which surprised me.
Vendrán mañana, *lo cual* **me gusta.**	They will arrive tomorrow, which pleases me.

4. Relatives that include the antecedent:
lo que, what (that which)

Me dijo *lo que* **pasó.**	He told me what happened.

Quien, -es (he who, those who; the one who, the ones who) are often used in place of *el que, la que, los que, las que.*

Quien **no estudia, no aprende.**	He who does not study, does not learn.
El que **no estudia, no aprende.**	

Cuanto, -a, -os, -as (all that, as much as, as many as) are often used in place of *todo lo que, todos los que,* etc.

Me dio *cuanto* **tenía.**	He gave me all that he had.

Cuyo, -a, -os, -as (whose) unlike the other relatives, is a possessive adjective and agrees in number and gender with the thing possessed (always the word that follows it).

¿Dónde está la niña *cuyo libro* **tengo?**	Where is the girl whose book I have?
Juan es el niño *cuyos padres* **están en Chile.**	John is the boy whose parents are in Chile.

24. Negatives

No always precedes the verb but may follow other words. Other negative words may precede or follow the verb, but if they follow, they must follow a negative verb (a double negative). The usual order is:

No + verb + another negative:

no   no, not
   Juan *no* **fue.**   John did not go.
   Ahora *no.* **Yo no.**   Not now. Not I.

nada   nothing, anything
   No **tengo** *nada.*   I haven't anything.
   Nada **tengo.**   I have nothing.

nadie   nobody, anybody
   No **fue** *nadie.*   ⎫
   Nadie **fue.**   ⎬ Nobody went.
   No **vi a** *nadie.*   I did not see anybody.
   No **dije** *nada a nadie.*   I did not say anything to any-

ninguno, -a   no, none   body.
(ningún)
   No **fue** *ninguno* **de ellos.** ⎫
   Ninguno **de ellos fue.** ⎬ None of them went.

   No **tiene** *ningún* **mérito.**   It hasn't any merit.
                        It has no merit.

tampoco   neither, either
   No **fue,** *ni* **yo** *tampoco.*   He did not go, nor did I.
   No **fui** *tampoco.*   ⎫
   Tampoco **fui.**   ⎬ I did not go either.

ni   nor
   No **lo he visto** *ni*
   quiero verlo.   I have not seen it nor do I
                        want to see it.

ni — ni   neither — nor
   No **tengo** *ni* **papel** *ni* **pluma.** ⎫
   Ni **papel** *ni* **pluma tengo.** ⎬ I have neither paper nor pen.

ni siquiera   not even
   Ni siquiera **me saluda.**   She does not even greet me.

nunca ⎫
jamás ⎬ never, ever

No me escribe *nunca* (jamás).	He never writes to me.
Nunca (jamás) me escribe.	Never does he write to me.
Nunca jamás le escribiré.	Never, never shall I write to him.

Note: *Nunca* means ever when it follows a comparative; *jamás* means ever when it follows an affirmative verb.

El canta mejor que nunca.	He sings better than ever.
¿Ha estado Ud. jamás en España?	Have you ever been in Spain?

Indefinite Adjectives and Pronouns

Indefinite Adjectives

uno (un), -a, -os, -as   a, an; some, a few
*alguno (algún), -a, -os, -as   some, any
ninguno (ningún), -a   no, not any

Recibió *unos* (algunos) regalos.	He received some gifts.
No recibió *ningún* dinero.	{ He received no money. / He did not receive any money.
Algunos barcos han llegado.	Some boats have arrived.
Ningún barco ha llegado.	No boat has arrived.

*Alguno, -a may be used in a negation, instead of *ninguno, -a*, if it follows a noun in the singular.

No es *ninguna* molestia.	} It is no trouble (at all).
No es molestia *alguna*.	

Indefinite Pronouns

alguien somebody, anybody	**uno (a-, -os, -as)** one, some
nadie nobody, anybody	**alguno (-a, -os, -as)** some, any
*algo something	(of a group in mind)
*nada nothing	**ninguno (-a)** none
	(of a group in mind)

Alguien le llama.	Somebody is calling you.
¿Ve Ud. a alguien?	Do you see anybody?
Nadie lo sabe.	Nobody knows it.
Tengo algo para Ud.	I have something for you.
No tengo nada para ella.	I have nothing for her.
Algunos son interesantes.	Some are interesting.
¿Vio Ud. a alguna de ellas?	Did you see any of them?
No vi a ninguna.	I did not see any of them.
Algunos de los soldados hablan francés.	Some of the soldiers speak French.
Ninguno de ellos habla inglés.	None of them speaks English.

*Note: *Algo* (somewhat) and *nada* (not at all) may also be used as adverbs.

María está algo mejor.	Mary is somewhat better.
El libro no me gusta nada.	I do not like the book at all.

Lo, ello, neuter: *Lo* is used to express an idea previously mentioned but not repeated. Sometimes it is translated as *it* or *so*. Many times it is not translated at all.

Dicen que es honrado, pero no *lo* **creo.**	They say he is honest, but I do not believe it.
Ana está enferma, pero no *lo* **parece.**	Anna is ill, but she does not look so.
¿Es María la tía del niño? Sí, *lo* **es.**	Is Mary the child's aunt? Yes, she is.

Ello (it) can also be used as the object of a preposition.

No estoy seguro *de ello.*	I am not sure of it.
Nunca consentirá *en ello.*	She will never consent to it.

25. Interrogatives and Exclamations

Interrogatives

Interrogatives are classified as adjectives, pronouns, and adverbs. They always have a written accent.

Adjectives and Pronouns

¿qué? what?
¿cuál, -es? which (one)? what?
¿cuánto, -a? how much?
¿cuántos, -as? how many?

¿quién, -es? who?
¿a quién, -es? whom? to whom?
¿de quién, -es? whose? of whom?

¿Qué libro tiene Ud.?	What book do you have?
¿Qué tiene Ud.?	What do you have?
¿Cuál es su libro?	Which is your book?
¿Cuál es el título?	What is the title?
¿Cuánto dinero tiene Ud.?	How much money do you have?
¿Cuánto tiene Juan?	How much does John have?
¿Cuántas primas tiene él?	How many cousins does he have?
¿Cuántas tiene Ud.?	How many do you have?
¿Quién sabe?	Who knows?
¿A quién vio Ud.?	Whom did you see?
¿A quién escribe María?	To whom is Mary writing?
¿De quién habla?	Of whom is he speaking?

Adverbs

¿cómo? how?
¿cuándo? when?

¿dónde? where?
¿por qué? why?

¿Cómo fue Ud.?	How did you go?
¿Cuándo volverá Juan?	When will John return?
¿Dónde viven?	Where do they live?
¿Por qué no fue Ud.?	Why did you not go?

Exclamations

Before adjectives or adverbs ¡qué! means what! or how!; before nouns it means what a . . . ! or what . . . ! After ¡qué . . . !, the indefinite article is not used. If a noun and an adjective are both used, the noun usually comes first and *tan* or *más* precedes the adjective. If the exclamation is a sentence rather than a phrase, the subject comes after the verb.

¡qué!	what!, what a!, how!
¡cuánto!	how!, how much!
¡cuántos, -as!	how many!
¡Qué suerte!	What luck!
¡Qué niño!	What a child!
¡Qué niña tan bonita! ⎫	What a pretty girl!
¡Qué niña más bonita! ⎭	
¡Cuánto me alegro!	How glad I am!
¡Cuántas flores hay!	How many flowers there are!

26. *Para & Por; Pero & Sino*

Para & Por

Para is used in the following cases: *para*   for, in order, by, about to

1. Use, for

tazas para té	teacups
vestidos para niñas	girls' dresses

2. Destination (person or place), for

La carta es para Concha.	The letter is for Concha.
El partió para Cuba.	He left for Cuba.

3. Purpose, in order

Estudia para aprender.	He studies in order to learn.
Trabajo para ganar dinero.	I work in order to earn money.

4. Point of future time, for, by

La lección para mañana	The lesson for tomorrow
Lo tendré para el lunes.	I shall have it by Monday.

5. *Estar para* + infinitive, to be about to

Juan está para salir.	John is about to leave.
Estaban para empezar.	They were about to begin.

Por is used in the following cases: *por*   through, along, by, per

1. Place through or along which

Pasó por el pueblo.	He passed through the town.
Andan por la acera.	They walk along the sidewalk.

2. Expressions of time, in, during, at

por la mañana, por la noche	in the morning, at night
por dos años, por mucho tiempo	for two years, for a long time

3. Exchange, price, for

Le di mi lápiz por su pluma.	I gave him my pencil for his pen.
Pagó un peso por el libro.	He paid a dollar for the book.

4. Unit of measure, by, per

Se vende por libras.	It is sold by the pound.
Gana cinco pesos por día.	He earns five dollars a day.

5. Way or means, by

Voy por tren.	I am going by train.
Lo hizo por fuerza.	He did it by force.

6. Because of, on account of, for

La ciudad es famosa por su clima.	The city is famous for its climate.

7. To go for, to send for, for

Voy por Alicia.	I am going for Alice.
Fue por un libro para mí.	He went for a book for me.

8. On behalf of, for the sake of, for

Lo hizo por su amigo.	He did it for his friend.
Voté por Eduardo.	I voted for Edward.

9. Motive, reason, for

Pelean por la libertad.	They are fighting for liberty.
No lo hizo por miedo al castigo.	He did not do it for fear of the punishment.

10. After a passive verb to indicate the agent, by

Fue escrito por Cervantes.	It was written by Cervantes.
Fue construido por los aztecas.	It was built by the Aztecs.

11. *Estar por* + infinitive, indicates what remains to be done to be in favor of

La carta está por escribir.	The letter is yet to be written.
Estoy por escribirla.	I am in favor of writing it.

Pero & Sino

Pero (mas), but, usually follows an affirmative expression, but may follow a negative statement if the verb of the first clause is repeated, or if another verb follows.

El es inteligente pero perezoso.	He is intelligent but lazy.
Bebe leche pero no bebe café.	He drinks milk, but he does not drink coffee.
Juan no bebe café pero bebe leche.	John does not drink coffee, but he drinks milk.

Sino, but, is used only after a negative in a constrasting statement when the verb of the first clause is understood but not repeated.

Juan no bebe café sino leche.	John does not drink coffee, but milk.

No sólo (solamente) . . . *sino también,* not only . . . but also

María no sólo toca el piano, sino canta también.	Mary not only plays the piano, but sings also.

27. Practical Rules

A Precedes a Personal Object

1. When the object of a verb (except *tener*) is a definite person or persons, it is preceded by *a,* which is not translated. It is not used, however, if a number precedes the object.

Veo *a Juan.*	I see John.
Veo *a los niños.*	I see the children.
Veo dos niños.	I see two children.
Juan tiene primos en España.	John has cousins in Spain.

2. The pronouns *alguien* (somebody) and *nadie* (nobody) although indefinite, require the personal *a* when used as the direct object of a verb. The same is true of *alguno, -a, -os, -as* (someone, some) and *ninguno, -a* (no one, none).

Veo *a alguien.*	I see somebody.
No veo *a nadie.*	I do not see anybody.
Veo *a algunas* **de ellas.**	I see some of them.
No veo *a ninguna* **de ellas.**	I do not see any of them.

3. *A* is used before geographical names except those that regularly require the article, such as *el Perú, el Brasil.*

Describió *a* **Chile.**	He described Chile.
No describió el Brasil.	He did not describe Brazil.

Possession

Ownership is expressed by *de* placed before the name of the possessor.

el libro *de Juan*	John's book
el perro *de los niños*	the children's dog
el gato *de la niña*	the girl's cat

The Infinitive as a Gerund

The infinitive is translated as a gerund when used with:

1. *El,* as a verbal noun,

El andar **es buen ejercicio.**
Walking is good exercise.

2. After *al,*

Al entrar, **vio a Alicia.**
On entering he saw Alice.

3. After a preposition,

Partió *sin verla.*
He left without seeing her.

4. After *ver* and *oír,*

Veo venir **a María.**
I see Mary coming.
Oigo cantar a María.
I hear Mary singing.

De, as with or in: After a past participle or an adjective, *de* is translated as with or in.

forrado de seda	lined with silk
lleno de alegría	filled with joy
cargado de leña	loaded with wood
cubierto de polvo	covered with dust
vestido de luto	dressing in mourning
Las montañas están cubiertas de nieve.	The mountains are covered with snow.

Que before *sí* or *no: Que* is used after *decir, creer,* and *esperar* when followed by *sí* or *no.*

decir que sí	to say yes	**creer que sí**	to believe so
decir que no	to say no	**esperar que no**	to hope not
Su madre dijo que no.	His mother said no.		
Creo que no.	I believe not.		
Espero que sí.	I hope so.		

Letter Changes

i to *y*

Unaccented *i* of a verb is changed to *y* when it occurs between vowels, unless it follows another *i,* in which case, one *i* is dropped.

leyó (for **leió**)	**cayendo** (for **caiendo**)
rió (for **riió**)	**riendo** (for **riiendo**)

o to *u*

The conjunction *o* is changed to *u* when it precedes a word beginning with *o* or *ho*.

siete u ocho **ayer u hoy**

o to *ó*

The conjunction *o* bears an accent when used between numbers.

2 ó 4, two or four

y to *e*

The conjunction *y* is changed to *e* when it precedes a word beginning with *i* or *hi*, but not *hie*.

padre e hijo	aguja e hilo	nieve y hielo
father and son	needle and thread	snow and ice

Words with and without the Written Accent

The written accent is used to distinguish words of the same spelling but different meaning.

aun even (one syllable)	**aún** still, yet
como as	**¿cómo?** how?
de of, from	**dé** from **dar**
el the	**él** he
mas but	**más** more
mi my	**mí** me
que than, that, which, who, whom	**¿qué?** what?; **¡qué!** What! how!
se reflexive pronoun	**sé** from **saber, ser**
si if, whether	**sí** yes, yourself, himself, etc.
solo alone	**sólo** only
te you	**té** tea
tu your	**tú** you

Aun los hombres tenían miedo.	Even the men were afraid.
No ha llegado aún.	He has not arrived yet.
Aún está lloviendo.	It is still raining.

Definite Article with Parts of the Body

The definite article is used when referring to the parts of one's body.

Me duele la espalda.	My back aches.
Elena tiene los ojos azules.	Ellen has blue eyes.

28. Suffixes

Suffixes may be added to almost any kind of word and they have many different meanings.

A suffix is usually added to the full form of a word ending in a consonant or an accented vowel. An unaccented vowel is dropped before the suffix is added. Some of the most commonly used suffixes are *-ito, -a* and *-cito, -a*.

These are diminutive forms and may indicate size, affection, admiration, appreciation, or pity.

Juan, Juan*ito* Johnny
hijo, hij*ito* little son
abuelo, abuel*ito* dear grandfather
papá, papa*íto,* **papa***cito* dear father
Ramón, Ramon*cito* little Raymond

libro, libr*ito* little book
pájaro, pajar*ito* little bird
chico, chiqu*ito* very small, a small boy
poco, poqu*ito* a small quantity
pobre, probre*cito* poor fellow
jardín, jardin*cito* little garden

Juana, Juan*ita* Jenny, Jean
hija, hij*ita* little daughter
abuela, abuel*ita* dear grandmother
mamá, mama*íta,* **mama***cita* dear mother
Carmen, Carmen*cita* dear Carmen
joven, joven*cita* young girl
mesa, mes*ita* small table
casa, cas*ita* small house
chica, chiqu*ita* very small, a small girl
cuchara, cuchar*ita* small spoon
pobre, pobre*cita* poor little thing

To indicate the maker, dealer, or one in charge of something, add *-ero, -a*.

la fruta, fruit, **frut***ero*
el jardín, garden, **jardin***ero*
la joya, jewel, **joy***ero*
la leche, milk, **lech***ero*
el libro, book, **libr***ero*

el pastel, pastry, **pastel***ero*
el rancho, ranch, **ranch***ero*
el reloj, watch, clock, **reloj***ero*
el sombrero, hat, **sombrer***ero*
el zapato, shoe, **zapat***ero*

To indicate the place where the article is made or sold, add *-ería*. The same result is obtained by adding *-ia* to the maker or dealer.

fruta, frut*ería* fruit store
joya, joy*ería* jewelry store
leche, lech*ería* dairy, place where milk is sold
libro, libr*ería* bookstore

pastel, pastel*ería* pastry shop
reloj, reloj*ería* watch or clock shop
sombrero, sombrer*ería* hat shop
zapato, zapat*ería* shoe store

These suffixes, *-ero, -era,* not only indicate the maker or dealer, but also the container of an article.

azúcar,	azucar*ero*	sugar bowl	leche,	lech*era*	milk pitcher
lápiz,	lapic*ero*	pencil-box	sombrero,	sombrer*era*	hat-box
pimienta,	piment*ero*	pepper-box	sopa,	sop*era*	tureen
sal,	sal*ero*	saltcellar	té,	tet*era*	teapot
tinta,	tint*ero*	inkstand	vinagre,	vinagr*era*	vinegar cruet

These suffixes, *-eza, -ura,* when added to an adjective, form abstract nouns.

grande,	grand*eza*	greatness	puro,	pur*eza*	purity
limpio,	limpi*eza*	cleanliness	triste,	trist*eza*	sorrow
alto,	alt*ura*	height	bravo,	brav*ura*	bravery
ancho,	anch*ura*	width	dulce,	dulz*ura*	sweetness
amargo,	amarg*ura*	bitterness	loco,	loc*ura*	madness

When these suffixes are added to a verb, *-dor, -a* with the final letter omitted, they indicate the performer of the action.

bailar to dance, baila*dor*	operar to operate, opera*dor*
cantar to sing, canta*dor*	patinar to skate, patina*dor*
comprar to buy, compra*dor*	pescar to fish, pesca*dor*
dictar to dictate, dicta*dor*	planchar to iron, plancha*dor*
educar to educate, educa*dor*	predicar to preach, predica*dor*
ganar to win, gana*dor*	trabajar to work, trabaja*dor*
jugar to play, juga*dor*	vender to sell, vende*dor*

29. Time

Days of the Week

lunes	Monday
martes	Tuesday
miércoles	Wednesday
jueves	Thursday
viernes	Friday
sábado	Saturday
domingo	Sunday

The days of the week are all masculine and are not capitalized. They are usually preceded by the definite articles and the preposition *en* (on) is not expressed.

el lunes	on Monday	**los lunes**	on Mondays

Hoy es lunes. — Today is Monday.

Voy a la playa el sábado. — I am going to the beach on Saturday.

Trabajo los sábados. — I work on Saturdays.

El domingo es día de descanso. — Sunday is a day of rest.

Months of the Year

enero	January	**julio**	July
febrero	February	**agosto**	August
marzo	March	**septiembre**	September
abril	April	**octubre**	October
mayo	May	**noviembre**	November
junio	June	**diciembre**	December

Seasons of the Year

la primavera	spring
el verano	summer
el otoño	autumn, the fall
el invierno	winter

The Date

The ordinal *primero* is used for the first of each month. For all other dates the cardinals are used.

¿Cuál es la fecha?
¿A cuántos estamos?   } What is the date?
¿Qué día del mes tenemos?

Es el primero de mayo (de 19 ___). It is the first of May, (19 ___).
Es el dos de mayo. El dos. It is the second of May. The second.

Estamos a primero de junio. It is the first of June.
Estamos a tres de junio. A tres. It is the third of June. The third.

Tenemos el primero de julio. It is the first of July.
  El primero. The first.
Tenemos el 10 de agosto de 19 ___ . It is the tenth of August, 19 ___ .

Buenos Aires, 4 de abril de 19 ___ . Buenos Aires, April 4, 19 ___ .
Se marchó el lunes, 6 de mayo. He left Monday, May 6.
Llegarán el día 4. They will arrive on the fourth.

Divisions of Time

el segundo   second
el minuto   minute
la hora   hour
media hora   half an hour
un cuarto de hora   a quarter of
  an hour
la mañana   morning
la tarde   afternoon

la noche   night
medianoche   midnight
el día   day
mediodía   noon
la semana   week
el mes   month
la estación   season
el año   year
el siglo   century

Expressions of Time

ahora   now
ahorita   right now
hoy   today
esta noche   tonight
anoche   last night
anteanoche   the night before last
mañana   tomorrow
pasado mañana   the day after
  tomorrow
por la mañana   in the morning
por la noche   at night
mañana por la mañana   tomorrow morning
ayer por la tarde   yesterday
  afternoon

ayer   yesterday
anteayer   the day before yesterday
la semana pasada   last week
la semana que viene }
la semana próxima } next week
el mes pasado   last month
el sábado pasado   last Saturday
el viernes próximo (que viene)
  next Friday
todo el día   all day
todos los días   everyday
todo el tiempo   all the time

Indefinite Time

a primeros del mes at the beginning of the month
a mediados del mes about the middle of the month
a últimos del mes toward the end of the month

a principios del año at the beginning of the year
a mediados del año about the middle of the year
a fines del año the latter part of the year

Time of Day

¿Qué hora es?	What time is it?
Es la una.	It is one o'clock.
Son las dos.	It is two o'clock.
¿A qué hora?	At what time?
A las cinco (en punto).	At five o'clock (sharp, exactly).

If it is not the exact hour, determine the nearest hour and then add or subtract the number of minutes, making the half hour the dividing point.

Es la una y veinte.	It is twenty minutes after one.
Son las nueve menos cinco.	It is five minutes before nine.
Son las ocho y media (de la mañana).	It is half past eight (in the morning). It is 8:30 (A.M.).
Son las cinco menos cuarto (de la tarde).	It is a quarter to five (in the afternoon). It is 4:45 (P.M.)
Son las once de la noche.	It is eleven o'clock at night. It is 11:00 P.M.

The Cardinal Points

el norte north
el sur, sud south
el este east
el oeste west

el nordeste northeast
el sudeste southeast
el noroeste northwest
el sudoeste southwest

30. Numerals

Cardinal Numbers

0 cero	27 veintisiete (veinte y siete)
1 uno (una, un)	28 veintiocho (veinte y ocho)
2 dos	29 veintinueve (veinte y nueve)
3 tres	30 treinta
4 cuatro	31 treinta y uno
5 cinco	32 treinta y dos
6 seis	40 cuarenta
7 siete	50 cincuenta
8 ocho	60 sesenta
9 nueve	70 setenta
10 diez	80 ochenta
11 once	90 noventa
12 doce	100 ciento (cien)
13 trece	200 doscientos, -as
14 catorce	300 trescientos, -as
15 quince	400 cuatrocientos, -as
16 dieciséis (diez y seis)	500 quinientos, -as
17 diecisiete (diez y siete)	600 seiscientos, -as
18 dieciocho (diez y ocho)	700 setecientos, -as
19 diecinueve (diez y nueve)	800 ochocientos, -as
20 veinte	900 novecientos, -as
21 veintiuno (veinte y uno)	1000 mil
22 veintidós (veinte y dos)	2000 dos mil
23 veintitrés (veinte y tres)	1.000.000 un millón (de)
24 veinticuatro (veinte y cuatro)	2.000.000 dos millones
25 veinticinco (veinte y cinco)	1.000.000.000 mil millones
26 veintiséis (veinte y seis)	1.000.000.000.000 un billón

Note: *Y* is used only to connect numbers from 16 through 99, however, the more popular spelling of the words for numbers 16 through 19 and 21 through 29 is to change the *y* to *i* and write the number as one word. Note that to retain pronunciation, the *z* of *diez* is changed to *c (dieciocho)*. Above 1000, numbers are expressed in thousands and hundreds, not hundreds.

165   ciento sesenta y cinco
1944   mil novecientos cuarenta y cuatro

A period is used to punctuate numbers: Large numbers are separated by a period, the comma being used to make the division between a whole number and a decimal.

1.453.674   1,453,672   **27,5**   27.5

Uno drops the *-o* before a masculine noun in the singular, and *-o* changes to *a* before a feminine noun. The compound numbers with *uno* also drop *-o* before masculine nouns, including the numerals *mil, millón,* and *billón.*

un libro   one book
veintiún libros   twenty-one
   books
treinta y un mil   thirty-one
   thousand

una pluma   one pen
veintiuna (veinte y una) plumas   twenty-one pens

Ciento drops *-to* before any noun, including the numerals *mil, millón,* and *billón.* The multiples of *ciento* must agree in number and gender with the nouns they modify.

cien libros   one hundred books
cien plumas   one hundred pens
cien mil   one hundred thousand
doscientos libros   two hundred
   books

cien buenos libros   one hundred
   good books
cien buenas plumas   one hundred
   good pens
doscientas plumas   two hundred
   pens

Odd and even numbers:

impar, non   odd
par   even

de dos en dos   by two's
de diez en diez   by ten's

**Los números nones son
3, 5, 7, etc.**
**Los números pares son
2, 4, 6, etc.**
**Cuente de cinco en cinco, de
cinco a cincuenta.**

The odd numbers are
3, 5, 7, etc.
The even numbers are
2, 4, 6, etc.
Count by five's from five to
fifty.

Collective Numbers

par *(m.)*   two, a pair
decena *(f.)*   ten, group of ten
docena *(f.)*   dozen
quincena *(f.)*   fifteen
veintena *(f.)*   twenty, a score

centena *(f.)* }
centenar *(m.)* } hundred

millar *(m.)*   thousand

Ciento and *mil* may be used in the plural as collective numbers.

centenares (cientos) de lagos
millares (miles) de ovejas

hundreds of lakes
thousands of sheep

Money:

100 céntimos = 1 peseta	(The value varies.)
100 centavos = 1 peso	(The value varies.)

Ordinal Numbers

1st **primero (-a, -os, -as)**	17th **décimo séptimo**
2nd **segundo**	18th **décimo octavo**
3rd **tercero**	19th **décimo noveno**
4th **cuarto**	20th **vigésimo**
5th **quinto**	21st **vigésimo primero (primo)**
6th **sexto**	22nd **vigésimo segundo**
7th **séptimo**	30th **trigésimo**
8th **octavo**	40th **cuadragésimo**
9th **noveno (nono)**	50th **quincuagésimo**
10th **décimo**	60th **sexagésimo**
11th **undécimo**	70th **septuagésimo**
12th **duodécimo**	80th **octogésimo**
13th **décimo tercero (tercio)**	90th **nonagésimo**
14th **décimo cuarto**	100th **centésimo**
15th **décimo quinto**	1000th **milésimo**
16th **décimo sexto**	

Ordinals may be abbreviated by using a figure and adding the last vowel of the word, 1°, 1ª, 2°, 2ª, etc. Ordinals agree in number and gender with the noun to which they refer. In the compound forms, both parts agree.

Primero and *tercero* drop the final -*o* if placed before a masculine singular noun. Ordinals may precede or follow the nouns. The compound forms usually follow.

el primer niño	the first boy	**la primera niña**	the first girl
el tercer libro	the third book	**el libro tercero**	the third book
la página décima sexta	the sixteenth page	**los primeros libros**	the first books

Fractions

1/2 **un medio** (adj.)	1/11 **un onzavo (once-avo)**
la mitad (noun)	1/12 **un dozavo, (doce-avo)**
1/3 **un tercio**	1/13 **un trezavo, (trece-avo)**
1/4 **un cuarto**	1/14 **un catorzavo, (catorce-avo)**
3/4 **tres cuartos**	1/20 **un veintavo, (veinte-avo)**
1/5 **un quinto**	1/21 **un veintiunavo, (veinte-y-**
1/6 **un sexto**	**un-avo)**
1/7 **un séptimo**	1/100 **un centavo, centésimo**
1/8 **un octavo**	1/1000 **un milésimo**
1/9 **un noveno**	
1/10 **un décimo**	

The fractions from 1-11 to 1-99 are formed by adding -*avo* to the cardinal number. The final vowel of the latter is usually dropped.

Fractions, beginning with 1-3, may be expressed by using the word *parte,* part, with an ordinal number:

1/3, la tercera parte; 1/4, la cuarta parte, etc.

Medio, half, is an adjective and agrees in gender with the noun to which it refers.

uno y medio	one and a half	**una hora y media**	an hour and a half
un peso y medio	a dollar and a half	**media libra de azúcar**	a half pound of sugar

Mitad, half, is a noun and does not change.

Perdió la mitad del dinero.	He lost half of the money.
La mitad de 4 es 2.	Half of 4 is 2.

Decimals

décima, -o	tenth	**centésima, -o**	hundredth
		milésima, -o	thousandth

9,3 nueve y tres décimas
12,05 doce y cinco centésimas
20,006 veinte y seis milésimas

Arithmetical Signs

+ *y, más*	**Adición**	$2 + 2 = 4$	**Dos y dos son cuatro.**
− *menos*	**Substracción**	$8-7=1$	**Ocho menos siete es uno.**
× *por*	**Multiplicación**	$2 \times 3 = 6$	**Dos por tres son seis.**
÷ *dividido por*	**División**	$6 \div 3 = 2$	**Seis dividido por tres son dos.**

= *es, son*

sumar	to add	**multiplicar**	to multiply
substraer, restar	to subtract	**dividir**	to divide

Dimensions

Tener is used to express dimensions *(tener . . . . de +* noun or adjective).

Nouns		Adjectives	
la altura	height	**alto, -a** high, tall	
la elevación			
la longitud	length	**largo, -a** long	
la extensión			
la anchura width		**ancho, -a** wide	
la profundidad depth		**profundo, -a hondo, -a** deep	
el espesor thickness		**grueso, -a** thick	

La torre tiene 50 metros de altura (alto).	The tower is 50 meters high.
¿Qué longitud tiene el río?	How long is the river?
El río tiene 500 millas de largo (longitud).	The river is 500 miles long.
La sala tiene 40 pies de anchura (ancho).	The room is forty feet wide.
Juan tiene seis pies de alto.	John is six feet tall.
El libro tiene dos pulgadas de espesor.	The book is two inches thick.

Ser + de is also used to express dimensions.

La anchura de la sala es de 15 pies.	The width of the room is 15 feet.

Units of Measure, Metric System

la hectárea	hectare	about 2½ acres
el kilo (kilogramo)	kilogram	a little over two pounds
el kilómetro	kilometer	about ⅝ of a mile
el litro	liter	a little over a quart
el metro	meter	39.37 inches

Other Units of Measure

la pulgada inch		la pinta pint
el pie foot		el galón gallon
la yarda yard		la libra pound
la milla mile		la tonelada ton

Geometrical Terms

Plane Surfaces:

la línea line	el rectángulo rectangle
el ángulo angle	el rombo rhomboid
el ángulo recto right angle	el círculo circle
el triángulo triangle	el diámetro diameter
el cuadrado, cuadro square	el radio radius

Solids:

el cubo cube	la pirámide pyramid
el cilindro cylinder	el cono cone
la esfera sphere	el prisma prism
el hemisferio hemisphere	

31. Letters

Names

A person's full name in Spanish consists of the given name, the father's family name and the mother's family name. The family names are usually joined by the conjunction *y,* but it may be omitted.

Antonio García y Moreno or **Antonio García Moreno**

If shortened, only the father's family name is used.

Antonio García

A woman, after marriage, keeps her family name, adding to it her husband's surname preceded by the preposition *de.**

Dolores García y Moreno becomes **Señora Dolores García de Torres**

If the woman is widowed, *viuda* is inserted.

Señora Dolores García Vda. de Torres.

*There is no equivalent form in Spanish for the abbreviation Ms., therefore, a woman's title still depends upon her marital status.

Parts of a Letter

el encabezamiento heading
la dirección ⎫
las señas ⎭ address
el saludo salutation
el fondo ⎫
el cuerpo ⎬ body
el contenido ⎭

la despedida ⎫
la conclusión ⎭ ending

la firma signature

la posdata postscript

Heading

Guadalajara, México
   4 de marzo de 19 __

Calle Mayor, 5
   Madrid, 3 de abril de 19 __

Nueva York, N. Y., 15 de mayo de 19 __

Santiago de Chile, 8 de enero de 19 __

Address

Señor Don Antonio Pérez	Sr. José Martínez
Calle del Arenal, 44	Calle de Sol, 15
Barcelona, España	Lima, Perú
Srta. Alicia Gutiérrez	Señora Doña Esperanza de López
Av. Madero, núm. 25	Calle Bolívar, 22
México, D. F.	Caracas
	Venezuela

Salutation

Business letters   For more formal letters

Muy señor mío:	Dear Sir:	Estimado señor:
Muy señores míos:	Dear Sirs:	Distinguido señor:
Muy señora mía:	Dear Madam:	Estimada señora:

Personal letters

Querido amigo:	Dear friend,
Querido Carlos:	Dear Charles,
Mi querida Carmen:	My dear Carmen,

Ending

Formal or Business Letters   Personal letters

De Ud. atto. y s.s.	
Su afmo. atto. y s.s.	Su amigo, Yours truly
Atto. y S. S.	Su afectísima amiga,
Quedo de Ud. s. s. s.	Tu prima que te quiere,
S. S. S.	

The following initials are often added to the customary endings:

Q. E. S. M. Used in writing to either a man or a woman
Q. B. S. M. to a man; **Q. B. S. P.,** to a woman.

Abbreviations

afmo., afma.	afectísimo, -a	very affectionate
atto., atta.	atento, -a	attentive
Av.	avenida	avenue
Cía.	compañía	company
D., Dn.	don	
Da.	doña	
Hos.	Hermanos	Brothers
no., núm.	número	number
P.D.	posdata	postscript
ptas.	pesetas	pesetas

Q.E.S.M. (q.e.s.m.)	que estrecha su mano	who shakes your hand
Q.B.S.M. (q.b.s.m.)	que besa sus manos	who kisses your hands
Q.B.S.P. (q.b.s.p.)	que besa sus pies	who kisses your feet
S.S. (s.s.)	seguro servidor	faithful servant
S.S.S. (s.s.s.)	su seguro servidor	your faithful servant
Sr.	señor	Sir, Mr.
Sres.	señores	Sirs, Gentlemen
Sra.	señora	Madam, Mrs.
Srta.	señorita	Miss
Ud., Vd., V.	usted	you
Uds., Vds., VV.	ustedes	you
Vda.	viuda	widow
1°, 2°, 3°, etc.	primero, etc.	first, etc.
7bre. or Sbre.	septiembre	September
pc/o. %	por ciento	per cent

32. Idioms

A

acabar de + inf. to have just completed the action of the inf.
aprovecharse de to avail oneself of, to profit by
a causa de because of
a eso de about
a fuerza de by dint of
a menudo often
al contrario on the contrary
al día siguiente the following day
al fin at last
al menos at least
al por mayor at wholesale
al mediodía at noon
al por menor at retail
al principio at first, at the beginning
a la derecha on or to the right
a la izquierda on or to the left

C

cambiarse de ropa to change clothing
casarse con to be married
cerrar con llave to lock
¡cómo no! of course!

D

dar a to face
dar con to meet, to come across
dar de comer to feed
dar las gracias to thank
dar un paseo to take a walk
darse cuenta de to realize
de buena gana gladly
de mala gana unwillingly
de día by day
de noche by night

de esta manera in this way
de ida y vuelta round trip
de la mañana in the morning; A. M.
de la noche in the night; P. M.
de la tarde in the afternoon; P. M.
de nada you are welcome
de par en par wide open
de parte de on behalf of
de prisa quickly
de repente suddenly
de rodillas kneeling
de vez en cuando from time to time
dejar de + inf. to cease; to fail to
dejar caer to drop

E

echar a perder to ruin
echar al correo to mail
echar de menos to miss, to feel the absence of
en seguida at once
estar a punto de + inf. to be about to
estar bien to be well
está bien all right
estar de pie to be standing
estar para + inf. to be about to

F

favor de + inf. please
fijarse en to notice

H

haber de + inf. to be to, to have to
hay que it is necessary

hay lodo   it is muddy
hay luna   the moon is shining
hay neblina   it is foggy
hay polvo   it is dusty
hay sol   the sun is shining; it's sunny

hacer

hacer buen tiempo   to be good
   weather
hacer mal tiempo   to be bad
   weather
hacer calor   to be warm
hacer fresco   to be cool
hacer frío   to be cold
hacer sol   to be sunny
hacer viento   to be windy
hacer un baúl   to pack a trunk
hacer una pregunta   to ask a
   question
hacer un viaje   to take a trip
hacerse daño   to harm oneself
hace mucho tiempo   a long time
   ago
hace poco   a short time ago
(haga Ud. el) favor de + inf.
   please
hoy día   nowadays

I

ir a casa   to go home
ir a la escuela   to go to school
ir a la iglesia   to go to church
ir de compras   to go shopping

J

jugar a la pelota   to play ball

LL

llegar a ser   to become
llegar a tiempo   to arrive on time
llevar a cabo   to finish

M

más que nunca   more than ever
mudarse de casa   to move
mudarse de ropa   to change one's
   clothing

P

pensar de   to think of, to have
   an opinion of
pensar en   to think about

perder cuidado   not to worry
poner en libertad   to set free
poner la mesa   to set the table
ponerse + adj.   to become
ponerse + article of clothing to
   put on
ponerse a + inf.   to begin
por consiguiente   consequently
por desgracia   unfortunately
por eso   therefore
por fin   at last
por lo menos   at least
por medio de   by means of
por supuesto   of course
por todas partes   everywhere
preguntar por   to ask about
   someone
probarse + article of clothing to
   try on

Q

¿Qué importa?   What does it
   matter?
¿Qué pasa?   What is the matter?
¿Qué tiene usted?   What is the
   matter?
querer decir   to mean
quitarse + article of clothing to
   take off

S

salir bien   to be successful
salir mal   to fail
sentar bien + ind. obj.   to fit well;
   to agree with
sentirse bien   to feel well
ser aficionado a   to be fond of
servirse de   to make use of
sírvase + inf.   please
soñar con   to dream about

T

tener años   to be . . . years old
tener buena suerte   to have good
   luck
tener mala suerte   to have bad
   luck
tener calor   to be warm
tener cuidado   to be careful
¡Tenga cuidado!   Be careful!
tener éxito   to be successful
tener frío   to be cold
tener ganas de   to desire

tener hambre to be hungry
tener la culpa to be to blame
tener lugar to take place
tener miedo to be afraid
tener prisa to be in a hurry
tener que + inf. to have to
tener razón to be right
tener sed to be thirsty
tener sueño to be sleepy
tener suerte to be lucky
tenga la bondad de + inf. please
¿**Qué tiene usted?** What is the
   matter?
aquí tiene usted here is
tocar + ind. obj. to be one's turn
tropezar con to meet, to come
   across

V

Vámonos Let us go
Vamos a ver Let us see
en voz alta in a loud voice
en voz baja in a low voice
por vez primera for the first
   time
volver a + inf. to repeat the action of the inf.

Vocabulary Lists

The American Republics

North American Republics

País Country	Capital Capital
los Estados Unidos	Wáshington, D. C. (Distrito de Columbia)
México	México, D. F. (Distrito Federal)

Cental American Republics

Guatemala	Guatemala
Honduras	Tegucigalpa
El Salvador	San Salvador
Nicaragua	Managua
Costa Rica	San José
Panamá	Panamá

South American Republics

Venezuela	Caracas
Colombia	Bogotá
el Ecuador	Quito
el Perú	Lima
Chile	Santiago
la Argentina	Buenos Aires
el Uruguay	Montevideo
el Paraguay	Asunción
Bolivia	*La Paz, Sucre
el Brasil	Brasilia

Island Republics

Cuba	la Habana
la República Dominicana	Santo Domingo
Haití	Port-au-Prince (Puerto Príncipe)

*Sucre, although the capital, is so inaccessible that La Paz is the center of government and administration.

Commonly Used Words and Phrases

Current Expressions

Buenos días. Good morning. Good day.
Buenas tardes. Good afternoon.
Buenas noches. Good evening. Good night.
¿Cómo está usted? How are you?
Muy bien, gracias. Very well, thank you.
¿Y usted? And you?
Hola. Hello.
Adiós. Good-bye
Hasta la vista. Until I see you.
Hasta mañana. Until tomorrow.
Hasta el lunes. Until Monday.

señor Mr., sir, gentleman
señora Mrs., lady
señorita Miss, young lady
Si, señor. Yes sir.
No, señor. No, sir.
(Haga Ud. el) favor de + inf.; **por favor** } please
¿Me hace Ud. el favor de ___ ? Will you please ___ ?
Con mucho gusto. With much pleasure.
Muchas gracias. Many thanks.
No hay de que. **De nada** } You're welcome.
Dispénseme. Excuse me.
Perdóneme. Pardon me.
Lo siento. I am sorry.

Languages and Nationalities

el inglés English
el español Spanish
el portugués Portuguese
el francés French
el latín Latin
el italiano Italian
el alemán German
el ruso Russian
el chino Chinese
el japonés Japanese

Commonly Used Words

el lápiz pencil
la goma eraser
la pluma pen
la plumafuente fountain pen
la tinta ink
el papel paper
el papel secante blotter
la carta the letter
el sobre envelope
el sello, timbre **la estampilla** } stamp
el cuaderno notebook
el libro book

Beverages

la bebida drink, beverage
el agua water
agua helada ice water
la leche milk
leche malteada malted milk
el café coffee
café solo black coffee
café con crema y azúcar coffee with cream and sugar
el té tea
el chocolate chocolate
el cacao cocoa
la limonada lemonade
la naranjada orangeade
el jugo de naranja orange juice
jugo de toronja grapefruit juice
el vino wine
la cerveza beer
la cidra cider

Food

el alimento food
algo que comer something to eat
el pan bread
el panecillo roll
la mantequilla butter
la carne meat
el pescado fish
las legumbres vegetables
la fruta fruit
el queso cheese

la galleta   cracker
los dulces   candy
el emparedado   sandwich
el helado   ice cream

Meats

la carne   meat
la carne de vaca (res)   beef
la ternera   veal
el carnero   mutton
el cordero   lamb
el cerdo (puerco)   pork
la chuleta, costilla   chop
la salchicha, el chorizo   sausage
el jamón   ham
el tocino   bacon
la lengua   tongue
el hígado   liver
el riñón   kidney

Fowl

la ave   fowl
el ganso   goose
el pato   duck
el pollo   chicken
el pavo, guajolote   turkey

Fish

el pescado   fish
el salmón   salmon
la trucha   trout
la sardina   sardine
el bacalao   cod
la langosta   lobster
la almeja   clam
el camarón   shrimp
la ostra   oyster

Vegetables

la legumbre   vegetable
la lechuga   lettuce
la col, el repollo   cabbage
la coliflor   cauliflower
los guisantes, chícharos   green peas
los espárragos   asparagus
la habichuela, el ejote   green bean
la espinaca   spinach
el tomate, jitomate   tomato

la zanahoria   carrot
el nabo   turnip
la remolacha, el betabel   beet
el apio   celery
la cebolla   onion
el pepino   cucumber
el perejil   parsley
la calabaza   squash
la alcachofa   artichoke
la berenjena   eggplant
el ruibarbo   rhubarb
el bróculi   broccoli
el berro   watercress
el elote   corn on the cob
el rábano   radish
el pimiento, chile   pepper
el ajo   garlic
la patata, papa   potato
la batata, el camote   sweet potato
las habas, judías }
los frijoles } beans

Fruit

la fruta   fruit
la manzana   apple
la naranja   orange
la banana, el plátano   banana
la toronja   grapefruit
el limón   lemon
la lima   lime
el melocotón, durazno   peach
el albaricoque   apricot
el higo   fig
un racimo de uvas   a bunch of grapes
la pera   pear
la ciruela   plum
la cereza   cherry
la piña   pineapple
el membrillo   quince
el melón   melon
la sandía   watermelon
la fresa   strawberry
la frambuesa   raspberry
la zarzamora   blackberry
el aguacate   avocado
el dátil   date

Cereals

el cereal   cereal
el trigo   wheat

el **maíz**   corn
el **arroz**   rice
la **avena**   oats, oatmeal
la **cebada**   barley
el **centeno**   rye

Meals

la **comida**   meal
el **desayuno**   breakfast
el **almuerzo**   lunch
la **comida**   dinner
la **cena**   supper
la **merienda**   light meal, snack
el **refresco**   refreshment

Menu

fruta fresca   fresh fruit
fruta cocida   stewed fruit
fruta de lata (bote)   canned fruit
huevos   eggs
_____ **fritos, tibios (pasados por agua)**   fried, boiled
_____ **revueltos**   scrambled
pan tostado   toast
mermelada   marmalade
(la) **miel**   honey
(el) **jarabe**   syrup
sopa   soup
_____ **de arroz**   rice
(el) **biftec, bistec**   beefsteak
carne de res asada
(el) **rosbif**   } roast beef
cocido, guisado   stew
(el) **puré de papas**   mashed potatoes
patatas al horno   baked potatoes
ensalada   salad
_____ **de lechuga**   lettuce
_____ **de legumbres**   vegetable
tomates rebanados   sliced tomatoes
salsa   dressing (sauce, gravy)
_____ **de mayonesa**   mayonnaise
_____ **francesa**   French
(el) **aceite de oliva**   olive oil
aceitunas   olives
mostaza   mustard

verduras   vegetables
(los) **postres**   desserts

helado   ice cream
_____ **de vainilla**   vanilla
_____ **de fresa**   strawberry

(el) **pastel**   pie, pastry
(el) **bizcocho, (la) torta**   cake
piña rebanada   sliced pineapple
conserva de fruta   preserves
compota de fruta   stewed fruit
pasas   raisins
(el) **flan**   custard
(las) **nueces**   walnuts

The Table

poner la mesa   to set the table
el **mantel**   tablecloth
la **servilleta**   napkin
el **tenedor**   fork
el **cuchillo**   knife
la **cuchara**   spoon
la **cucharita**   teaspoon
el **plato**   plate, dish
el **vaso**   glass
la **taza**   cup
la **sal**   salt
el **salero**   saltshaker
la **pimienta**   pepper
el **pimentero**   pepper shaker
el **azúcar**   sugar
el **azucarero**   sugar bowl
el **vinagre**   vinegar
la **vinagrera**   vinegar cruet
la **cafetera**   coffeepot
la **tetera**   teapot
la **bandeja, charola**   tray

The Human Body

la **cabeza**   head
el **pelo, cabello**   hair
el **cráneo**   skull
la **cara**   face
la **frente**   forehead
la **ceja**   eyebrow
la **pestaña**   eyelash
el **ojo**   eye
el **párpado**   eyelid
la **oreja**   ear
la **nariz**   nose
la **mejilla**   cheek
el **cutis, la piel**   skin
la **boca**   mouth
el **labio**   lip
la **lengua**   tongue

el diente   tooth
la barba   chin
el cuello   neck
la garganta   throat
el tronco   trunk
el hombro   shoulder
los brazos   arms
el codo   elbow
la muñeca   wrist
la mano   hand
el dedo   finger
la uña   nail
la espalda   back
el pecho   chest
el pulmón   lung
el corazón   heart
el estómago   stomach
el hígado   liver
el riñón   kidney
la pierna   leg
la rodilla   knee
el tobillo   ankle
el pie   foot
el dedo del pie   toe
el talón   heel
el hueso   bone

The Family and Relatives

la familia   family
el esposo, marido   husband
la esposa, mujer   wife
los padres   parents
el padre   father
la madre   mother
los hijos   children
el hijo   son
la hija   daughter
el hermano   brother
la hermana   sister
el abuelo   grandfather
la abuela   grandmother
el nieto   grandson
la nieta   granddaughter
los bisabuelos   great-grand-
   parents
los bisnietos   great-grandchildren
los parientes   relatives
el tío   uncle
la tía   aunt
el sobrino   nephew
la sobrina   niece

el primo, la prima   cousin
el suegro   father-in-law
la suegra   mother-in-law
el cuñado   brother-in-law
la cuñada   sister-in-law
la nuera   daughter-in-law
el yerno   son-in-law
el padrastro   stepfather
la madrastra   stepmother
el hijastro   stepson
la hijastra   stepdaughter

The House

la casa   house
la entrada   entrance
la puerta principal   front door
la sala de recibo   living room
el gabinete   den, study
el comedor   dining room
la cocina   kitchen
la alcoba, recámara ⎫
el dormitorio   ⎬ bedroom
la habitación, el cuarto   room
el armario   closet, wardrobe
el cuarto de baño   bathroom
la chimenea   fireplace, chimney
la escalera   stairway
la pared   wall
el suelo   floor
el techo   ceiling, roof
el tejado   roof
el pasillo   hall
la ventana   window
el piso bajo   ground floor
el primer piso   second floor

Furniture

el mueble   furniture
la mesa   table
la mesita   small table
el diván, el sofá   couch, sofa
el escritorio   desk
la silla   chair
el sillón, la butaca   armchair
el estante para libros   bookcase
la alfombra   carpet, rug
el tapete   rug
la cortina   curtain, drape
la lámpara   lamp
el cuadro   picture

el **aparador**   buffet
el **guardarropa, ropero**   wardrobe, clothes closet
la **cama**   bed
el **tocador**   dresser
la **cómoda**   chest of drawers
la **estufa**   stove
el **refrigerador**   refrigerator

The Bed

el **colchón**   mattress
la **sábana**   sheet
la **almohada**   pillow
la **funda**   pillowcase
la **manta, frazada**   blanket
la **colcha**   spread

The Dressing Table

el **espejo**   mirror
el **peine**   comb
el **cepillo para el pelo**   hairbrush
el **cepillo de dientes**   toothbrush
el **dentífrico**   dentifrice
los **polvos (el polvo)para la cara**   face powder
la **crema para la cara**   face cream
la **loción**   lotion
el **perfume**   perfume
el **lápiz para los labios**   lipstick
el **colorete**   rouge
la **horquilla**   hairpin
el **alfiler**   pin
_____ **de seguridad**   safety pin
la **navaja de rasurar (afeitar)**   razor

Clothing

la **ropa**   clothing
prendas de vestir   articles of clothing
los **vestidos**   clothes
el **vestido**   dress
el **traje**   dress, suit
la **blusa**   blouse
la **falda**   skirt
la **chaqueta**   jacket
el **abrigo**   wrap, coat
el **sombrero**   hat
la **boina**   beret

un **par de medias**   a pair of stockings
los **zapatos**   shoes
las **zapatillas, pantuflas**   slippers
la **bata**   dressing gown, robe
la **ropa interior**   underwear
los **guantes**   gloves
la **bolsa**   purse, handbag
los **chanclos**   overshoes, galoshes
el **impermeable**   raincoat
el **paraguas**   umbrella
el **uniforme**   uniform
el **pantalón, los pantalones**   trousers, slacks
el **chaleco**   vest
el **saco, la americana**   coat
la **camisa**   shirt
el **cuello**   collar
la **corbata**   tie
el **cinturón**   belt
los **tirantes**   suspenders
el **calcetín**   sock
el **pañuelo**   handkerchief
la **gorra**   cap
el **sobretodo, gabán**   overcoat
la **cartera**   wallet, billfold
los **calzoncillos**   shorts
el **pijama**   pajamas

Animals

el **animal**   animal
el **caballo**   horse
el **potro**   colt
la **vaca**   cow
el **becerro, ternero, -a**   calf
el **toro**   bull
el **buey**   ox
la **mula**   mule
el **burro**   donkey
la **oveja**   sheep
el **cordero**   lamb
la **cabra**   goat
el **cabrito**   kid
el **perro**   dog
el **gato**   cat
la **rata**   rat
el **ratón**   mouse
el **conejo**   rabbit
la **ardilla**   squirrel
los **pollos**   chickens
el **gallo**   rooster

la gallina hen
los pollitos chicks
el pavo, guajolote turkey
el pato duck
el ganso goose
la tortuga turtle
la rana frog
el sapo toad
el pájaro bird
el canario canary
el loro parrot
la paloma dove, pigeon
el águila eagle
la golondrina swallow
el gorrión sparrow
el león lion
el tigre tiger
el elefante elephant
el camello camel
la jirafa giraffe
el venado deer
el oso bear
el lobo wolf
la zorra fox
el mono monkey
el rinoceronte rhinoceros
el hipopótamo hippopotamus
el pez fish
la ballena whale
el tiburón shark
el caimán alligator
la serpiente, culebra serpent
el gusano worm

Insects

el insecto insect
la mariposa butterfly
la abeja bee
la hormiga ant
la araña spider
la mosca fly
el mosquito mosquito
la pulga flea
la polilla moth
la cucaracha cockroach
la chinche bedbug
la langosta grasshopper

The Garden

el jardín garden
la flor flower

el ramo de flores bouquet
la rosa rose
el clavel carnation
la violeta violet
el pensamiento pansy
la orquídea orchid
la gardenia gardenia
la camelia camellia
el crisantemo chrysanthemum
el lirio lily
la dalia dahlia
la margarita daisy
el geranio geranium
el narciso narcissus
el jazmín jasmine
la madreselva honeysuckle
la amapola poppy
el tulipán tulip
la capuchina nasturtium
la nomeolvides forget-me-not

Trees

el árbol tree
el roble, la encina oak
el pino pine
el cedro cedar
el nogal walnut
la caoba mahogany
el arce maple
la palmera palm
el olivo olive tree
el naranjo orange tree
el manzano apple tree
la higuera fig tree
el cerezo cherry tree
el castaño chestnut tree
el álamo poplar

Studies

la asignatura subject or
  course of study
la historia history
las matemáticas mathematics
el álgebra algebra
la geometría geometry
la ciencia science
la física physics
la química chemistry
la zoología zoology
la botánica botany

la geografía   geography
la música   music
el arte   art
el dibujo   drawing
la pintura   painting
la teneduría de libros   book-
   keeping
la taquigrafía, estenografía
   stenography
la mecanografía   typing
la gimnástica   physical training

The City

la ciudad   city
la calle   street
la acera, banqueta   sidewalk
la avenida   avenue
el paseo   boulevard
la plaza   square
el parque   park
la manzana, cuadra   block
la estación de ferrocarril   railroad
   station
el muelle   dock, pier
el aeropuerto   airport
el hipódromo   race track
el estadio   stadium
el cementerio, camposanto   cem-
   etery

Buildings

el edificio   building
la casa comercial   business house
la tienda   store, shop
la fábrica   factory
el banco   bank
el hotel   hotel
el café   café
el teatro   theater
el cine   movie theater
la casa de ayuntamiento   city
   hall
la casa de correos, el correo
   post office
el buzón   mailbox
la comisaría   police station
la cárcel   jail
el hospital   hospital
la biblioteca   library
el museo   museum
el palacio   palace

la casa particular, (privada)
   private house
la casa de apartamientos   apart-
   ment house
la escuela   school
la universidad   university
la iglesia   church
la catedral   cathedral

Stores, Shops

la tienda de comestibles
   (abarrotes)   grocery store
el mercado   market
la carnicería   meat market
la panadería   bakery
la papelería   stationery shop
la confitería, dulcería   candy shop
la droguería, farmacia, botica
   drugstore
la cantina   bar
la librería   bookstore
la sastrería   tailor shop
la zapatería   shoe shop
la barbería, peluquería   barber
   shop
el salón de belleza   beauty parlor
la tintorería   dyer's, cleaner's
la lavandería   laundry

Transportation

el automóvil   automobile
el tranvía   streetcar
el tren   train
el barco   boat, ship
el buque de vela   sailing vessel
el vapor   steamer
el avión, aeroplano   airplane
el taxi   taxi
el camión   truck, bus
el ómnibus   bus
la bicicleta   bicycle
la motocicleta   motorcycle

Journey, Trip

el viaje   trip
la estación   station
el despacho de billetes (boletos)
   ticket office
el billete sencillo   one-way ticket
_____ de ida y vuelta   round trip

el equipaje baggage
el baúl trunk
la maleta suitcase
facturar to check
el talón check
el asiento seat
el conductor (revisor) conductor
el pasaporte passport
la aduana customhouse
el mozo porter
la propina tip
el horario, la guía timetable
la locomotora engine
el coche cama pullman
el coche comedor dining car
¡Señores viajeros al tren! All
  aboard!

The Hotel

la oficina office
el gerente manager
el empleado employee
el dependiente clerk
el mozo bellboy
firmar, inscribirse to register
la habitación, el cuarto room
el baño bath
_____ de regadera, la ducha
  shower
_____ de tina tub
el agua caliente hot water
la toalla towel
la pastilla de jabón bar of soap
el ascensor, elevador elevator
la llave key
cerrar con llave to lock
la cuenta bill
el cajero cashier
la caja cashier's desk or office

Professions and Trades

el médico doctor
el dentista dentist
el oculista oculist
el abogado, licenciado lawyer
el profesor, catedrático professor
el maestro teacher
el predicador preacher
el padre, cura priest
el ingeniero engineer

el arquitecto architect
el escritor writer
el periodista journalist
el actor actor
la actriz actress
el músico musician
el pintor painter
el boticario, farmacéutico pharmacist
el comerciante merchant
el banquero banker
el fotógrafo photographer
el carpintero carpenter
el plomero plumber
el zapatero shoemaker
el carnicero butcher
el panadero baker
el sastre tailor
el barbero, peluquero barber
el mecánico mechanic
el tenedor de libros bookkeeper
el dependiente clerk
el vendedor salesman
el viajante traveling salesman
el electricista electrician
el florista florist
el cartero postman
el policía, agente de- policeman
el soldado soldier
el marinero sailor
el aviador aviator, flyer
el piloto pilot
la secretaria secretary
la taquígrafa, estenógrafa stenographer
la mecanógrafa typist
la modista dressmaker
la enfermera nurse

Titles

el emperador emperor
la emperatriz empress
el rey king
la reina queen
el virrey viceroy
el marqués marquis
la marquesa marchioness
el conde count
la condesa countess
el duque duke

la duquesa   duchess
el sultán   sultan
la sultana   sultana
el presidente   president
el vicepresidente   vice-president
el gobernador   governor
el alcalde   mayor
el papa   pope
el cardenal   cardinal
el obispo   bishop
el general   general
el coronel   colonel
el capitán   captain
el teniente   lieutenant
el sargento   sergeant
el cabo   corporal
el almirante   admiral
el alférez   ensign

la península   peninsula
el cabo   cape
el golfo   gulf
la bahía   bay
el océano   ocean
la costa   coast
la playa   beach
el mar   sea
el río   river
el lago   lake
la montaña   mountain
el valle   valley
la llanura   plain
el desierto   desert
la selva   jungle
el bosque   forest
el istmo   isthmus

Metals

el oro   gold
la plata   silver
el cobre   copper
el hierro   iron
el acero   steel
el bronce   bronze
el estaño   tin
el plomo   lead
el platino   platinum
el aluminio   aluminum
el níquel   nickel

Materials

el ladrillo   brick
la madera   wood, lumber
la piedra   stone
el mármol   marble
el vidrio   glass
el hule, caucho   rubber
el yeso   plaster
la seda   silk
el algodón   cotton
la lana   wool
el lino   linen, flax

Geography

el continente   continent
la isla   island

Sports

la pelota   ball
el balompié, futbol   football
el beisbol   baseball
el basquetbol   basketball
el tenis   tennis
la natación   swimming
la piscina, alberca   pool
el boxeo   boxing
la lucha   wrestling
las carreras   races
jai alai   jai alai
la corrida de toros   bullfight
el deporte   sport
el juego   game
el partido   match, game
el equipo   team
el jugador   player
el boxeador   boxer
el luchador   wrestler
el matador   bullfighter

The Car

el coche   car
manejar, guiar, conducir   to drive
la estación de servicio   service
   station
el garage   garage
el tanque   tank
la gasolina   gasoline
el aceite   oil
el aire   air
la grasa   grease

engrasar to grease
el neumático, la llanta tire
llanta picada punctured tire
_____ de repuesto spare
la rueda wheel
el volante steering wheel
el freno brake
estacionarse to park
la velocidad speed
despacio slow
peligro danger
alto stop
siga, adelante go

Polite Phrases

¡Felicitaciones! Congratulations!
Feliz viaje. Pleasant trip.
Felices vacaciones. Pleasant vaca-
  tion.
Felices Pascuas.} Merry Christmas
Feliz Navidad.
Feliz Año Nuevo. Happy New Year.
Buena suerte. Good luck.
Que se divierta Ud. Have a good
  time.
Igualmente. The same to you.

Holidays

(la) Navidad Christmas
Día de Navidad Christmas Day
Nochebuena Christmas Eve
Día de Año Nuevo New Year's
  Day
Semana Santa Holy week, Easter
  week
Viernes Santo Good Friday
Domingo de Resurrección Easter
  Sunday

Index

Verb Index

This verb index will enable you to compare hundreds of commonly used verbs with the book's numerous verb tables. Each group of verbs provides page numbers where particular tenses are given, and a comprehensive list of common regular verbs that follow those patterns. By recognizing which verbs follow a certain pattern, you will greatly increase your vocabulary and fluency—all at a glance. Each verb group also includes a list of common irregular verbs, followed by page numbers you can consult for irregular conjugations.

-*ar* Verbs

The -*ar* verbs constitute by far the largest verb group in Spanish. The good news is that the vast majority of -*ar* verbs—including the most common ones—are regular. Tip: pay special attention to common idiomatic verbs like *gustar*, *faltar*, and *sobrar*, where the subject and object roles are the reverse of English.

Regular -*ar* Verbs

Regular -*ar* verbs are conjugated following the pattern of *hablar*. The various conjugations of *hablar* can be found on the following pages:

infinitive, 7	future perfect, 15
present, 8	conditional perfect, 16
imperfect, 11	present subjunctive, 20
preterite, 11	past subjunctive, 21
future, 11	present perfect subjunctive, 22
conditional, 12	past perfect subjunctive, 22
past participle, 14	gerund, 33
present perfect, 14	progressive tenses, 33–34
past perfect, 15	imperative, 52
preterite perfect, 15	

Some common -*ar* verbs:

acabar to finish	**aconsejar** to advise
aceptar to accept	**adivinar** to guess, figure out
acercarse** to approach	**admirar** to admire
aclarar to clarify, explain	**adorar** to adore
acompañar to accompany	**agarrar** to grasp, grab

agitar   to shake, stir
agotar   to exhaust, use up
aguantar   to put up with, tolerate
ahorrar   to save
almacenar   to store
almorzar*   to lunch
alquilar   to rent, hire
amar   to love
anunciar   to announce, advertise
apagar**   to extinguish
apartar   to remove, set aside, stray
aportar   to contribute, provide
apostar*   to bet, wager
apoyar   to support, lean, second
  (a motion)
apreciar   to appreciate, perceive
aprovechar   to take advantage of,
  make the most of
arreglar   to arrange
asegurar   to assure, make sure
asustar   to frighten, scare
aumentar   to increase, rise
averiguar**   to ascertain
avisar   to warn, tell
ayudar   to help
bailar   to dance
bajar   to go/bring down, lower
besar   to kiss
borrar   to erase
calcular   to calculate, work out
cambiar   to change, exchange
caminar   to walk
cancelar   to cancel, settle
cantar   to sing
castigar**   to punish
causar   to cause
celebrar   to celebrate, praise
cenar   to have dinner
charlar   to chat
citar   to make an appointment,
  quote
cobrar   to cash, charge
cocinar   to cook
colaborar   to collaborate, contribute
colgar*   to hang
colocar**   to place
comprar   to buy
conectar   to connect
contar*   to count
contestar   to answer
controlar   to control
cortar   to cut
crear   to create, invent

cuidar   to look after, care for
cultivar   to grow, cultivate
dejar   to leave, let, forget
desarrollar   to develop, explain
desayunar   to have breakfast
descansar   to rest
desear   to wish, desire
despertar(se)*   to awake
dibujar   to draw
disfrutar   to enjoy, have a good time
doblar   to fold, double, turn, dub (film)
dudar   to doubt
durar   to last, continue
echar   to throw, throw out, give off
educar**   to educate
emplear   to use, employ
empujar   to push
engañar   to deceive, trick
engordar   to make/get fat, put on
  weight
enseñar   to teach, show
entrar   to enter
entregar**   to hand over, give
envidiar   to envy
escuchar   to listen
esperar   to hope, wait
estudiar   to study
exagerar   to overdo, exaggerate, go too
  far
experimentar   to experience, feel, test
explicar**   to explain
expresar   to express, show
extrañar   to surprise, miss
fabricar**   to manufacture
facilitar   to facilitate, get, provide
faltar***   to miss, not to go, be
  lacking/needed
felicitar   to congratulate, compliment
figurar   to appear, figure, be important
firmar   to sign
formar   to form, give shape, make (up)
fracasar   to fail
fumar   to smoke
funcionar   to function, work (machine)
ganar   to earn, win, gain
gastar   to spend, use up, wear out
gritar   to shout
guardar   to keep, put away, take care
  of
gustar***   to like
hablar   to talk
importar***   to be concerned about
indicar**   to indicate

iniciar   to initiate, begin
interesar***   to interest, concern
invitar   to invite
jugar*   to play
juntar   to join, unite
jurar   to swear, take an oath
lavar   to wash
limpiar   to clean
llamar   to call
llegar**   to arrive
llenar   to fill, fill out/up/in
llevar   to carry, take, wear
llorar   to cry
lograr   to get, achieve
luchar   to fight, struggle
madrugar   to get up early
mandar   to order, send, command
manejar   to manage, handle, drive
marcar**   to mark
matar   to kill
mejorar   to improve
mirar   to look at
molestar   to annoy, bother
montar   to ride, get on, set up
nadar   to swim
navegar**   to navigate
necesitar   to need
obligar**   to compel
observar   to observe, notice
odiar   to hate
olvidar   to forget
ordenar   to straighten up, order, ordain
parar   to stop, stay
pasar   to pass, happen, spend time
pegar**   to beat, stick
pensar*   to think
pintar   to paint, describe
pisar   to step, stand on
plantar   to plant, throw
preguntar   to ask
preparar   to prepare
presentar   to introduce, present
prestar   to lend, give
procurar   to try, get
pronunciar   to pronounce
publicar**   to publish

quemar   to burn
quitar   to take off/away, remove
reaccionar   to react
reformar   to reform, improve
regalar   to give (as a gift), give away
regar*/**   to water, irrigate
regresar   to return, come/go back
relacionar   to relate, connect
renunciar   to renounce
reparar   to repair, notice
resultar   to result, turn out, be
retirar   to remove, withdraw, retire
robar   to steal, rob
sacar**   to take out
saltar   to jump, leap
saludar   to greet, salute
secar**   to dry
sentar(se)*   to seat, sit
señalar   to point to, point out, mark
separar   to separate, move away, set aside
significar**   to mean, signify
sobrar***   to be/have left over, have more than enough
soportar   to bear, stand
sospechar   to suspect, think
subrayar   to underline, emphasize
sumar   to add up, amount to, summarize
tardar   to take (time), be a long time, delay
terminar   to finish
tirar   to throw, pull, spill
tocar**   to touch, play (musical instrument)
tomar   to take, have (drink or food)
trabajar   to work
transformar   to transform, become
tratar   to deal with, treat, try, be about
usar   to use
valorar   to value, appreciate
viajar   to travel
vigilar   to watch, keep an eye on
visitar   to visit
votar   to vote

---

*Radical-changing verb: See pages 45–46.
**Orthographic-changing verb: See pages 49, 51.
***Used in third-person singular and plural with indirect object pronoun: See pages 60–61.

Irregular *-ar* Verbs

Next are some common *-ar* verbs with irregular conjugations, which can be found on the following pages:

alcanzar   to reach, 39
andar   to go, 35
aplazar   to postpone, 39
comenzar   to begin, 39
confiar   to trust, 41
continuar   to continue, 41
criar   to raise, rear; 41
cruzar   to cross, 39
dar   to give, 36

empezar   to begin, 39
enviar   to send, 41
estar*   to be, 36
guiar   to guide, 41
lanzar   to cast, 39
organizar   to organize, 39
vaciar   to empty, 41
variar   to vary, 41

*For common uses of **estar** (vs. **ser**), see pages 43–44.

-er Verbs

Although this verb group is smaller than the *-ar* group, it has many irregular verbs. Tip: pay special attention to the most common of these irregular verbs, such as *conocer, hacer, tener, poder, querer, saber,* and *ser.*

Regular *-er* Verbs

Regular *-er* verbs are conjugated following the pattern of *comer.* The various conjugations of *comer* can be found on the following pages.

Note: Conjugations of *hablar* are provided for perfect and progressive tenses, since in these cases all regular *-ar*, *-er*, and *-ir* verbs are conjugated alike.

Some common -er verbs are:

aprender to learn	**esconder** to hide
barrer to sweep	**meter** to put, put in
beber to drink	**mover*** to move
ceder to cede, yield, hand over	**ofender** to offend, insult
coger** to catch	**oler*** to smell
comer to eat	**perder*** to lose
comprender to understand	**proteger**** to protect
convencer** to convince	**recoger**** to collect, gather
correr to run	**recorrer** to go/travel through, cross
creer to believe, think	**resolver*** to resolve
deber to owe	**responder** to answer
depender to depend	**someter** to subdue, submit
disolver* to dissolve	**sorprender** to surprise
doler* to hurt	**suceder** to succeed, happen
ejercer** to exercise	**temer** to fear
emprender to undertake, embark upon	**torcer(se)*/**** to twist
	toser to cough
encoger** to shrink	**vender** to sell
escoger** to choose	**volver*** to return

*Radical-changing verb: See pages 45–46.
**Orthographic-changing verb: See page 50.

Irregular -er Verbs

Next are some common -er verbs with irregular conjugations, which can be found on the following pages:

agradecer to thank, be grateful; 39	**ofrecer** to offer, 39
aparecer to appear, 39	**oler** to smell, 37
caber to be contained, fit; 35	**permanecer** to remain, 39
caer to fall, 35	**pertenecer** to belong to, 39
conocer to know, be acquainted with; 39	**poder** to be able, 37
crecer to grow, 39	**poner** to put, place, 37
desaparecer to disappear, 39	**querer** to wish, want, love; 37
establecer to establish, 39	**reconocer** to recognize, 39
haber to have, 36	**saber** to know, 37
hacer to do, make; 36	**ser*** to be, 38
merecer to deserve, 39	**tener** to have, 38
obedecer to obey, 39	**traer** to bring, 38
	valer to be worth, 38

*For common uses of **ser** (vs. **estar**), see pages 43–44.

-ir Verbs

Again, this verb group is smaller than the -ar group, but it has many irregular verbs (though not as many as the -er group). Tip: pay special attention to the most common irregular verbs, such as *decir, ir, oír, salir,* and *venir.*

Regular *-ir* Verbs

Regular *-ir* verbs are conjugated following the pattern of *vivir*. The various conjugations of *vivir* can be found on the following pages.

Note: Conjugations of *hablar* are provided for perfect and progressive tenses, since in these cases all regular *-ar*, *-er*, and *-ir* verbs are conjugated alike.

Some common *-ir* verbs are:

abrir   to open (irregular past participle: *abierto*)
acudir   to come, go
admitir   to admit, allow
advertir*   to warn
asistir   to attend
compartir   to share
competir*   to compete
conseguir**   to obtain
consentir*   to consent
convertir*   to convert
corregir*/**   to correct
cubrir   to cover
cumplir   to fulfill, keep one's word, be _____ years old (birthday)
decidir   to decide
describir   to describe
descubrir   to discover (irregular past participle: *descubierto*)
despedir(se)*   to take leave of
dirigir**   to direct
discutir   to argue
distinguir**   to distinguish
dividir   to divide, separate
dormir*   to sleep
elegir*   to choose, elect
escribir   to write (irregular past participle: *escrito*)

exigir**   to demand
extinguir**   to extinguish
fingir**   to pretend
impedir*   to prevent
insistir   to insist, emphasize
interrumpir   to interrupt, cut off/short
medir*   to measure
mentir*   to lie
morir*   to die
ocurrir   to occur
partir   to divide, share, leave
pedir*   to ask for
permitir   to permit, let
perseguir**   to pursue
preferir*   to prefer
recibir   to receive
reír(se)*   to laugh
repartir   to distribute, share, deliver
repetir*   to repeat
sacudir   to shake, beat
seguir**   to continue, follow
servir*   to serve
sonreír*   to smile
subir   to climb, go up
sufrir   to suffer, undergo
suprimir   to suppress, omit
surgir   to arise, come up

transmitir   to convey, get across   vestir(se)*   to dress
unir   to unite, join, combine   vivir   to live

*Radical-changing verb: See pages 46–47.
**Orthographic-changing verb: See page 50.

Irregular *-ir* Verbs

Next are some common *-ir* verbs with irregular conjugations, which can be
found on the following pages:

atribuir   to attribute, 40
concluir   to conclude, 40
conducir   to conduct, 40
constituir   to constitute, 40
decir   to say, 36
deducir   to deduce, 40
destruir   to destroy, 40
excluir   to exclude, 40
huir   to flee, 40
incluir   to include, 40

instruir   to instruct, 40
introducir   to introduce, 40
ir   to go, 36
oír   to hear, 37
producir   to produce, 40
reducir   to reduce, 40
reñir   to quarrel, scold; 41
salir   to go out, leave; 38
traducir   to translate, 40
venir   to come, 38